LEADER
most LOVED

Inspire Productive, Loyal Teams...and Become a **Leader Worth Following**

LEADER
most LOVED

Inspire Productive, Loyal Teams...and Become a **Leader Worth Following**

ASHTON UNDERDAHL, PMP

Published by Best Seller Publishing®, St. Augustine, FL
Best Seller Publishing® is a registered trademark.
Printed in the United States of America.
ISBN: 978-1-956649-92-5

For more information, please write:
Best Seller Publishing®
53 Marine Street
St. Augustine, FL 32084
or call 1 (626) 765-9750
Visit us online at: www.BestSellerPublishing.org

EARLY PRAISE FOR
LEADER MOST LOVED:

"Ashton's advice is clinically sound; utilizing positive reinforcement, the sandwich method, implementing a self-care plan and much more!"

–Katrina Barker, MS, Licensed Professional Counselor

"Ashton provides a pathway for new leaders and young professionals to quickly increase their business acumen. She also provides guidance on how to manage the demands of work and life, and that guidance is critical. Any first time or second time manager; any leader or small business owner; anyone looking to improve professionally or personally should read this book."

—Melissa Lesley, Project Management Professional

"Ashton delivers practical guidance for a foundation of healthy lifestyle, work satisfaction, and physical exercise backed by science. At the same time, she captures the essence of what every leader should strive to be!"

—Kyle McCrite, MS, Licensed Occupational Therapist, Registered

DEDICATION

This book is dedicated to my team, who poured out their love for me and inspired me to share my story as a young professional in small business. My hope is that this book is your guiding light to many years as a Leader Most Loved and that you might adore your team as much as I do.

I would like to thank my mentors for believing in me and trusting me as a young professional. I would like to thank my mother, Cindy, who taught me everything I know about running a business and working hard, and Jodie, for having my back and treating me like a partner. I would like to recognize Susan, Jackie, and Brenda for building me up. I would like to thank my coaches, Lisa and Barbara for instilling positivity in me. Lastly, I would like to thank my husband, Scott for always supporting my dreams. I love each of you and I would not be who I am without you.

CONTENTS

Early Praise for Leader Most Loved v

Dedication vii

Introduction xi

Part 1: The Foundation **1**

   1: Self-Management is the Expectation 3

   2: 1+1=3, Right? 13

   3: Positivity is King 27

   4: Recognition is Queen 37

Part 2: The Studs **47**

   5: Communication 49

   6: Goals and Your Team 63

   7: Red Pill, Blue Pill 73

   8: Take me to Tahiti 83

Part 3: The Finishing Touches **93**

   9: What's Your Water Cooler? 95

   10: Drink the Kool-Aid 103

   11: It's All About Me Now (Well, You) 117

   12: Time Management is my Superpower 127

So, What Now? 139

Scenarios 143

INTRODUCTION

Over the past fifteen to twenty years, I have learned a great many lessons on how to lead a team. To love a family you weren't born into and lead a company to greatness; many lessons were learned through failure and trial. You spend more time with your work family than you do your actual family, and that's important to recognize. As the leader of your organization, your department, or your project team, it is very important to nurture those relationships and ensure a healthy workplace under your leadership, especially if it's a virtual one. Your role is ultimately to create a workplace where people want to spend time together. Your team should thrive on your business's vision and believe in the work they're doing together. That will ensure that your team is happier at work – and so are you! In this book we will explore several concepts that you can learn to live by to become a loved leader. If you are a manager, young leader, or a small business owner, this book is for you. Hopefully after reading this book, you get to skip a bunch of failures and trials, gain from my experience and journey, and nurture those healthy working cultures inside your business, department, or team!

As a child, I was a Junior Olympic gymnast. I had incredibly supportive and loving parents, who helped me get to up to twenty-four hours of practice each week. They were very hard working and ambitious people and instilled a diligent work ethic in me. They pushed me to be the best version of myself and to give the glory of it all to God. Inside my gymnastics environment, I was coached by the most positive individuals I've ever met – genuinely. The gym was literally a "no negatives" environment. They pushed us hard, physically and mentally, but loved us every moment of practice. They nurtured our positivity and therefore, our motivation. I retired from gymnastics in the elite levels due to a broken lumbar spine in my mid-teens, and had life-changing surgery, a lumbar fusion. But my gymnastics family still loved me, and I became a coach. They continued to foster my positive coaching techniques, and my parents continued to support my passion for the sport I loved. Even after I left for college, I still coached gymnastics in other cities, and the children I coached are still my Instagram friends to this day.

I am a natural coach but became a leader of a business by accident. I was drawn to organizing the chaos and professionally grew up inside my organization – I think my years of coaching children may have spurred that. Being in a small company, I gained a lot of responsibilities very early on in my career. By the time I became a manager, I had quickly recognized that I was surrounded by experts with decades of experience on me. I feared letting them down, or worse; offending them – so I made my job, from that point forward, to become their humble servant. I would be the springboard the staff and clients needed – to grow the rest of the organization. This belief catapulted me into executive leadership, and each of the departments knew they could count on me to expand their skills, motivate them, believe in them, and allow them to grow in a safe place where they felt valued. When you breed a culture of empowered people, your people don't leave. People are happy to come to work and be there with you for years.

I began my career young, starting out as an administrative assistant during my freshman year of college. Back then, the company I worked for only had three employees, including me. I opened mail and filed it, I answered phones and emails. As I learned the business, I was trusted with more. I began screening employment candidates and training new hires on our procedures. I managed the contracts and productivity of our independent contractors, managed inquiries from clients regarding accounts, turn-around times, and requests for new business. We were growing. Before we knew it, it was time to expand.

In the last two years of my undergraduate degree, I traveled to see clients across the nation with a group of peers. Some of them had been in the business ten and twenty years already, though some were greener just like me. I had a knack for organizing tasks and humans, and quickly became central to the team. We were taking on so many projects and clients that the need for project management quickly became apparent. I earned my Certified Associate of Project Management (CAPM) credential and presented my case for business to my leaders; we needed a Project Manager position and Project Management service offerings to ensure the success of our projects, and I was going to be the one to lead it. They agreed, and from there, I created our first Project Management Office. It was instantly our most profitable offering, but most importantly, the PMO became the central cog of our services wheel. If the team needed a problem solved, direction or information, they came straight to me. The group had grown by double, and as I mentioned, many of my peers had anywhere from ten to twenty years of expertise on me. It was intimidating at times, and I often felt out of my league, but recognizing how exceptional my peers were early on is what saved my bacon.

I then earned my Project Management Professional (PMP) certification to hone my skills and prove my value to the team and our leaders. With the infrastructure I helped design, we began bringing new Project Managers and Project Specialists, and even Technical Specialists into the organization.

These Specialists were smarter than me, and that gave me more motivation to ensure that I was someone they could count on. I attended webinars, registered for newsletters, met with colleagues, shadowed clients and other professionals, and ensured I stayed in the know – enough to keep pace with them and reassure them that I was someone they could trust to back them up. They had deep expertise on the applications we were providing services in. In order to keep them on my side, and meet the customers' needs, I became their launch pad. I learned about them, professionally and personally. I offered my assistance and guidance when it was appropriate. I earned their trust.

After a change in ownership at our small company, I was prepared for anything, including being let go. To my surprise, I was promoted to Chief Operating Officer (COO). I was just twenty-nine years old. I was accountable for all departments, services, functions, processes, and our people. It was a great honor to lead the company I loved so much. The company was thriving, and so was I.

Once trust was the foundation of the relationship, management was easy. I had never set out to be a manager of people per say, but my devotion to the team propelled it. My expectation of each team member was self-management, a can-do attitude, and communication. Both employee and manager had precisely what they needed. In not-too-distant history, my small company was acquired by a huge one. This is a large company that I still very much adore, and I'm often in contact with its people. Upon the acquisition, I was transitioned into a Director role over the team that has been acquired. People at the new company frequently told me how "rare" I was as a leader. I had multiple new hires ask me if I was for real. *"Is working here really like this?" "Are you really this nice?" "Your team is really something you don't see in the corporate world."* I knew we had something special, and I started to recognize that we might have a recipe to share with other teams.

Unexpectedly, after thirteen years in my career, I hit a pothole. I had developed Pelvic Congestion Syndrome where blood was pooling in my pelvis, and I could no longer sit at my desk for those long days. The gymnastics surgery (a lumbar fusion), two pregnancies and a devotion to my career created the perfect storm in my body, and I was forced to re-evaluate my priorities. This was a very difficult time as working hard and having a fruitful career was part of my identity.

My boss and I spent weeks trying to figure out ways for me to stay; I even had a panic attack trying to come to terms with my reality. Ultimately, there was only one answer – it was time to focus on my health. But, to my surprise, my team loved me anyway. They sent me flowers; they threw me a dinner party. Our new COO bought me a watch; my Vice President hand-made me a gift basket. They sent me farewell cards. My boss wrote me a note that said *"You are amazing. You have mentored our team and me to a great place. We are set up for success due to you. Love you."* Months after I resigned, we were still meeting for lunch or dinner; we had done the impossible and moved beyond the manager/employee relationship and simply had a relationship based on mutual respect and fondness. A few of the memos I received were...

For all the years I've known you, I couldn't express my gratitude for helping me navigate work and life through all of the ups and downs. You have played such a huge role in my life and the last 8+ years I truly can say you were the most kind, caring, and supportive person. I wish you nothing but the best and want to THANK YOU for literally everything. I wouldn't be here today without you, especially in my career. I'll always admire you.

Ashton, you will truly be missed. Thank you for giving me this opportunity 6 years ago. I am eternally grateful and will love you always.

Love you long time, Ashton. Work will not be the same without you. Thank you so much for your amazing leadership and guidance.

Thank you, Ashton, for immediately making me feel like part of the family from day one. You have helped me grow in so many ways and I am truly grateful for the honesty, guidance, support, and inclusion you have always given me. I will miss you so much and will always think of you when I use our nicknames.

Good luck, Ashton! You will be so missed. So thankful to learn from you.

There are no words to express how much I adore you. You were my mentor and my friend. We all will carry on all the learning, laughs, and love you brought to our team. I love you.

I love you so much! I can't thank you enough for everything you've done for me. Because of you I am where I am. I wouldn't have been able to grow my career or as a person. You took me out of my tight shell and made me more comfortable and confident to continue to grow! Thank you for everything.

We wish you well, Ashton! Here's a little something to show our appreciation for your hard work and dedication.

From 2019–2021, I was the Vice President of Finance, and then the President of a local Project Management Institute chapter. I served for 2.5 years and as my term finally ended, one month after I resigned from my position, I unexpectedly received thank you's from each board member.

"You are so amazing. Your leadership and friendship have been lifechanging – not only to me, but to our membership."

"Thank you for your leadership – you will be missed." and "Thank you for all you have done."

"Thank you for your stellar leadership." and "Thank you for your service and your leadership."

"I have learned so much from you and will keep in touch."

I thought I would quietly ride off into the sunset; I wasn't expecting these kinds of goodbyes. I was so humbled by these words from people I respected so much, that I knew I had to share what I'd learned from my experiences and help others put these principles into practice.

In this book, I will share twelve incredibly important methods I've developed over the past twenty years that will lead you to be a well-loved, effective leader. Implementing these methods will enable you to create a healthy, positive, trusting, and happy business organization in just a matter of months – management will become simpler, business will flow easier, employees will be better served, and your clients will notice, too. I hope that from the findings of my personal journey you can gain experience, as well as management and leadership techniques, learn the unsaid in hiring, reduce overhead costs, expect better business outcomes, create a happier work culture (virtual or not!), create a more productive and loyal team (and therefore generate more revenue!), and finally, become a Leader Most Loved.

PART 1

THE FOUNDATION

1

SELF-MANAGEMENT IS THE EXPECTATION

The Foundation Lesson 1: Self-Management is the Expectation

I've always been drawn to leadership and team building. I was a class officer every year of high school, and in college, I was Co-President of my class program. While I possessed the talent and desire, my skills were not yet harnessed. In fact, as a young Project Specialist, I became central to problem-solving as my organization and follow through skills were superior, but I believe at one point my boss called me an "ankle-biter" – like a dog with a bone. A passion for organizing the chaos is what fostered my operational expertise, but with it came people management which was less natural to me. I became a leader by grand-design, but a manager of people unintentionally – it came with the territory. While I love people, I loathe *managing* people. I am naturally a lover and a coach, so disciplining employees was very tough for me in the beginning. No one enjoys confrontation. We all like passing out carrots and no one wants to wield that stick! When I was first given management responsibilities, I was the youngest team member. It was extremely intimidating. Given this, and my natural dislike for discipline, I made it quite clear to the team, and all candidates wanting to be on the team, that I expected self-management. I implemented this self-management philosophy initially because I didn't want these experts feeling like I was telling them how to do their job or that I was stepping in their camp, but the more I grew as a manager and a leader, the more I learned how effective this concept is as a total people strategy. For some managers, relinquishing the day-to-day control to your team is absolutely terrifying (and if you don't have the right team in place, could be impossible or dangerous!). It does require a great deal of trust, and a time or two, I was taken advantage of but ultimately, it was worth the gamble, and I'm about to break down exactly why.

What People Want.

In my experience, a consistent theme when conducting interviews with candidates or asking employees about their past experience is that they felt over-managed, micromanaged, or felt that they had little freedom in their position. When you approach managing your team with a self-management expectation, the employee feels empowered to make decisions that positively affect their career. It is a more transparent and personal transaction. As a manager, it also enables you to manage to their strengths whenever possible and minimize their weaknesses. It also helps simplify any PIPs (performance improvement plans) you might have to complete in the future. Don't worry if this sounds intimidating right now; we will discuss leveraging strengths and using skills matrixing as part of a healthy manager/employee relationship in part two.

What is Self-Management?

It sounds appetizing right out of the gate, right? Most of the time, this is what the employee wants too – but it's not for everyone. Self-management is not code for a hands-off manager, or for a closed off relationship with your manager either. It's actually code for accountability, for both the manager and the employee. Occasionally, that requires explanation.

- As a manager utilizing the self-management expectation, I indicate to my team I expect them to manage their own time, plan out their own days and weeks, own their goals, run their tasks and manage their own job processes.
- I expect they will communicate with me when they anticipate a hurdle, or any other indication that they will have a roadblock preventing them from moving forward with expected activities, as well as when things are going according to plan.
- I expect that I will not have to follow up on their activities, but that they are addressing their productivity independently.
- I expect that schedule changes are managed and communicated; and that they are reliable.
- I expect that they value their work and their time and, I expect they know they have my respect and trust.

The trajectory of their career is entirely in their hands; they are driving the car and I am riding shotgun. I will hold the map, give directions, and pass them the snacks – anything and everything they need from me while they drive the car.

Self-management is not code for a lazy manager either. This style of management does not mean less work and is not a cop out for ineptitude. Of course, I do follow up on the activities and productivity of the whole team and so should you – we are trying to run a business after all! When you are not constantly micromanaging your team however, it opens up time for you to understand and meet your team where they are at, and understand each individual within the team. Understanding where your team is and how each individual is a component of it is a huge part of maintaining the self-management philosophy's infrastructure. You should also take the time to know their job processes and tasks, even if only at the highest level. You should know, and make time to know on a regular basis, how many projects your Project Managers have, how many widgets are backlogged for Team 3, how many units we shipped as a team last week, how many tickets are in the helpdesk queue... you get the picture. Understanding your department's (and company's if they differ) units of productivity factor into every piece of the revenue scheme – how much each position is paid, how much revenue was generated or lost, what overhead we tolerate, etc. You should know what each position is capable of, has the potential for, and where your employee lands on those spectrums. In addition to these more technical components of management, you should take the time to know each team member individually; how they perform in their position, which aspects bring them joy (or distress), and what aspects of their role bring them satisfaction.

If you've become a manager of a team where self-management was not an expectation, slowly begin implementing small parts of the method that are comfortable and tolerable. Start with one person, one metric, then move on to another when you see successes. Now, let's jump into exactly how to implement this.

How Do I Implement It?

Start by reviewing your team's job descriptions. If you don't have them yet, start making them. If you are starting from scratch, review them with the HR representative, your superior, or your business coach, and then the employee. Get them signed off on and agreed upon by all parties. By reviewing the job descriptions, you understand what their intended responsibilities are and how they vary from their actual responsibilities. Which pieces are they doing? Not doing? Why? Does the current job description meet the needs of this position?

Complete your analysis and note your remarks. Compare the job descriptions to your company's goals or the goals you are accountable for. Observe how are they connected (or disconnected!).

Then, discuss the position's responsibilities with the employee. It's time to get their feedback! Ask them which pieces of the job description they are actually pursuing now and which pieces they aren't, and why. Come to an agreement on changes if there are significant disconnects or discrepancies. Then, have them walk you through a workday in their life. What does their position look like on a day-to-day basis? What tasks do they perform and on what interval? What processes do they use to complete their tasks? Go into as much detail as is required for you to understand what they're going through. Even consider job-shadowing your pros to fine-tune your understanding.

Lastly, ask what goals they have for their position or career, documenting as you move along. Your objective in asking is to understand what motivates them, satisfies them, and see what alignment those goals have with the department or company.

Ask how they are used to being managed, and what they like or dislike about it. Make sure to take notes and stay engaged. Start explaining to your team that you are trying to empower the whole team to perform their tasks independently. Your goal is for them to gain some autonomy and by gathering this level of detail you can have total trust that the team has all components accounted for. Share your philosophy on self-management and what working with you as a manager is going to feel like (see Scenario D in the back of the book for more help). Describe your desire to form a partnership with them.

Set up regular communication intervals with each individual, as well as the team (we will discuss those in part two, also). Start each relationship off on the right foot and take a little time to get to know them. Depending on how many changes you must implement, or how many processes you have to change, you might need to incrementally implement self-management techniques to avoid disrupting productivity.

Continue to meet with everyone on your team one at a time, and monitor progress towards self-management benchmarks. Remember, lots of little steps will add up to big progress! Deploying this strategy reduces the guesswork associated with management in your position and allows you to focus on investing in the team to grow the company.

What to Do with This Strategy

- Do show them respect right out of the gate. Let them know you are here to serve and your desire is successful outcomes for all.

- Do show them your intentions, and highlight that you plan to have a partnership with them. Let them know you want to see them in the driver's seat of their career, and you'll be right beside them. Self-motivated and independent operators will do extremely well with this sort of interaction! Let them know you want to be involved in their workday and be a supportive role to their position; but that they will be in charge of their trajectory.

- Pay attention to any red flags from your team. If you have already sensed an accountability issue, giving them more rope could worsen the situation. You will have to determine what you and your team can cope with. I was once told "keeping the bad apple rots the whole farm." Self-Management as a people strategy is essentially two-way trust. Make sure it's actually two-way. To see how to deal with this strategy backfiring, see Scenario I in the back of the book.

- Keep excellent documentation. Avoid making handshake deals. Keep a record of what's discussed and agreed upon, and make sure it aligns with what is in the employment agreement or if modifications are required.

Who will Struggle in This Kind of Environment?

Newer employees or those newer to the career field might struggle with this in the beginning. They might need the direction of a manager or mentor in order to start their day. In other words, they aren't able to clearly see priorities on their own, or turn the bigger picture goals into individual tasks. That's okay – we all go through learning cycles, but it's something that you'll need to keep tabs on and make a plan to manage. Without a plan to get these types of employees to self-management, they may feel like they are throwing darts at a dart board or, even flounder under "lack of direction". Providing them structure to get started will be paramount to their success.

I once had an employee who fired himself. We had previously discussed with him issues regarding timeliness and procrastination, accomplishment and productivity needing to meet expectations. Finally, he simply told me, "I just can't do this. I can't self-manage while working from home. All I want to do is wander over to the living room and play video games." And that was okay – we helped him get hired at his next employer.

Employees with more thoughtful or compliant communications style might be afraid of this model at first. In fact, autonomy might sound isolating, rather than empowering. They might even feel alienated or like they are being setup to fail – if that's the case, you need to back up the bus and make sure that's NOT what you are doing. Reveal the pieces that are making them uncomfortable and make a plan for it by reviewing the job description and your analysis with them. Co-manage it with them for a period of time to ensure they get comfortable and will be successful. Lastly, very direct team members may mistake servant leadership or components of self-management as a lack of confidence. You will need to match their directness with candidness regarding your approach to proceed successfully. Detail your expectations with assertion to communicate effectively to them.

What Day-to-Day Employee Self-Management on a Team Looks Like:

A professional team comprised of individual self-managers is usually a very efficient and happy one. Why? Because the whole team knows they can trust one another to do their part. Because they are a team, they work together for the good of the group; and therefore, take more pride in their work. Each team member is able to be accountable for their pieces and to the team. People like to be counted on and valued. Day-to-day, problems or roadblocks are communicated out loud so the team can rally to resolve them quickly. It's your duty to foster this mentality and promote prompt communication within your department, which we will discuss at length in part two.

So, How's This Managed?

- Employee manages individual tasks, projects, and processes, and owns their own pieces.
- Employee is accountable to their team and for their outcomes.
- Manager has the foresight to know what the employee is going through and respect's the employee's expertise.
- Manager manages to results and outcomes.
- Employee and Manager communicate and agree on the roles and outcomes.

RECAP The Foundation Lesson 1: Self-Management is the Expectation

1. Ensure you understand the expectations of your staff and that they understand your role.
2. Get to know your staff, inform of expectations, and agree to expectations.
3. Incrementally implement self-management practices.
4. Give trust to get trust.
5. Evolve into Self-Management Total People Strategy.

Reflection Question:

What does it feel like to have you as a manager? How you will you describe the implementation of self-management principles to your team?

_____

_____

_____

_____

_____

_____

_____

_____

_____

_____

_____

_____

_____

_____

_____

Notes:

_____

_____

_____

_____

_____

_____

_____

_____

_____

_____

_____

_____

_____

_____

_____

_____

_____

_____

_____

_____

_____

_____

_____

2

1+1=3, RIGHT?

The Foundation Lesson 2: 1+1=3, Right?

You know, math never was my best subject. In fact, in a very rebellious moment in 8th grade, I wrote "I don't do math" on the top of my homework. Needless to say, I didn't get an "A" in that class.

It's true; one plus one does not equal three, especially in hiring. When picking the right candidates for your team, the following qualities are the only things that adds up to three: Skills, Experience, and Character. The right quantity of these three qualities is what makes your perfect candidate. Based on the job description and your team, you need determine how much you need in each area in what I call the Talent Triangle of hiring.

Character is the moral and ethical mental state of a candidate. Character is completely unique to each candidate and only you and your team decide what components will mesh well in your corporate culture, what we can accommodate, or what the business is unable to tolerate. Skills are what a candidate has been taught through schooling or on-the-job training. More skills can be learned, and often they are represented by credentials and certificates. Experience is expertise gained through years of exposure. Often times, experience is more valuable than skills to me as an employer, for a couple reasons. I may be specifically looking for a pro, who can run circles around me and take the department to a new high; or I might be looking for a rookie who we can really groom and grow together in a different way. Overall, each role will need a different combination of the Talent Triangle, and it's your job to uncover what that intersection of character, experience, and skills looks like for each hire.

I love hiring. At one time, I even thought I might want to be a recruiter because it's so satisfying to find the right candidate and watch as they settle right into the perfect role. It's extremely important that you hire with intention and sincerity. I have made desperation hires where I ignored my red flags, and every single time (with no exception) it backfires. Your gut will never lie to you; and one plus one *never* equals three.

Finding candidates with the right experience or enough skills to get started is rarely the issue; those things can be taught or earned.

Don't know Python that well? Great, take a training course. Fresh out of school? Let's get you set up with a mentor. One thing that cannot be taught, however, is integrity. It's very unlikely you can modify character; you cannot change a person's core being or their principles. It's more important that those fundamentals in a candidate align with you and your business.

When hiring, I always tailor the job description to exactly what we need. Don't just recycle the same job descriptions before thinking about what you need for that role and your team currently. Before you post it, document the qualities you need in a candidate. Is it punctuality? Is it enthusiasm? What's the ideal communication style for the position you are posting? Use two to four screening questions in the application to avoid drawing out the interview process. If you are able, use an additional screening tool like a personality test or a communication style questionnaire, or even LinkedIn Quizzes if you need too. It's incredibly helpful to get to know a person with a little bit more than just the resume. Lastly, show the salary range! It will save everyone, especially you, very valuable time.

Now, if the candidate got to the point of actually interviewing with you, they clearly have the skills and/or experience you are looking for – the interview is really your shot to get to know them as a person, to uncover their character. Try interviewing with a peer or department leader to get multiple perspectives. I always ask questions that will reveal their character, their intention, their values, and their communication style. I use multiple choice questions to see how a candidate uses the process of elimination, and to see if they share with me why they chose the way they did. I want to hear about how they see themselves in team settings and how they react in certain scenarios. I want to hear how they get their work done and the expectations they have of themselves. I also need a glimpse into what kind of human they are and if they are going to be a successful addition to the current team. I need to fall in love with the person they are so they can be part of the team for years to come!

Here are some of my absolute favorite questions to ask in an interview. There are also several personality tests and communication style assessments that you can and should rifle through to compile your very own interview questionnaire that really works for you.

- When you walk into the conference room, do you sit at the head of the table, where others can see you, next to someone else, or near the far edge of the table?

This question tells me what type of communication style they might have in a business setting. If they want to sit at the head of the table, they might have a tendency to lead, or they might have a tendency to "steal the show" and you need a follow up question to decipher which. I prefer to use behavioral or situational questions to help reveal which it may be. If they want to be where people can see them but not at the head, they might be an analyzer and less of a situational driver. If they sit next to someone, they may be more thoughtful or team-oriented person or feel isolated by independence; while on the other hand, if they sit at the edge of the table away from others, they may prefer independence over teamwork; or it could even be lack of confidence. Dig in! Think about the position they are applying for. Which is most appropriate for the circumstances in that role?

- Which word do you value the most? Which word do you value the least? The words are: Team, Challenge, Appreciation, Feedback, Recognition, Independence.

Did they take the time to tell me why? Did they describe any of the other words? Do the words they choose align with what I am hiring them for? Which words would the rest of your team select? Which words would you say? This question helps me understand if they are applying for the right role and how they are going to interact in a team environment. It will also reveal how competitive or direct they can be in work settings.

- What are your top three favorite songs?

This one almost always throws people off, but how they answer will tell you a lot about them. Remember, they already sweated through the screening process and made it to an interview with you, so we are really trying to dive into what type of person they are. It became a crowd favorite amongst my hiring team very quickly. It also clues the candidate into what kind of manager I am; I care about more than just the work getting done. This question often reveals how the candidate views themselves, maybe how they like to spend their time...it's a glimpse into who they are outside the office.

- What are three things that you want in this position, that would make you stay here?

During an interview, you usually learn what scorched them before or caused them to apply for this position right away — we learn from that. How is this situation different for this person? Part of a holistic leader/team member relationship is understanding expectations. You must know what motivates them, and what they will be expecting from you and from the role.

- How do you make a tough decision? Do you look at how others will be affected by it, do you rely on your own judgement, do you seek the approval of others prior to deciding, or do you rely on specific methodologies to make the decision?

This question reveals pieces of their communication style, but also how they are going to work with a team, as well as their capacity to lead. Again, think about the position you are hiring them for. What do you expect from them in terms of decision-making capabilities? I have changed how this question is presented to candidates several times over the years; you can also try multiple choice, or changing it to a situational question.

- A client calls you and is very upset with how Jennifer processed the reports this month. The client claims there were typos, inaccurate date ranges, and a data point was completely missing. How do you respond?

I have used this question in multiple choice format also, but other times I just want to listen. I don't want to lead them to the answer I want just yet; I want to see what part of their character is revealed right now. Will they cover it up and just fix it? Will they take notes and pass it to their supervisor? Will they grab their teammate to hop on the phone with them? What would you want a member of your team to do in this circumstance?

- What are your top three strengths that would bring value to the team? What are your top three weaknesses?

A time-tested question; I want to see how they view themselves and how honest they are willing to be with me. Being able to put your faults on the table is difficult and makes you feel vulnerable. Acknowledging their strengths and weaknesses is also a sign of greater intelligence, philosophically and emotionally.

What are Communication Styles?

Understanding your employees and superiors' communication styles will single-handedly change the ball game for you. If you understand people's communication styles, you can tailor your communication accordingly, and break down all barriers to collaboration while getting a better glimpse into their character. I have used several different communication style assessments (The HRDQ assessment, and the DISC assessment, and the TTI Insights); and even worked with my team to create our own. Try a few on your own! Determine which of these works for you or develop your own. Regardless of which assessment you choose, there tend to be four communication styles, which I'll break down for you here.

1. Direct (also called Dominance or Candid)

This type of communicator might make decisions quickly, skip greetings in emails, and might come across as stern or confident. When you are exchanging with a Direct communicator it's best to stay professional, focus on the facts, and try to be face to face (or video to video) so you get the most of out of the transaction. A lot of entrepreneurs have this communication style due to their tendency to take charge. Because Direct communicators don't often express emotion, they tend to get along best with Systematic communicators, might unintentionally offend Thoughtful communicators, and could be annoyed by Enthusiastic communicators.

2. Enthusiastic (also called Influence)

This type of communicator is convincing, passionate, animated, friendly, and likes to be in close spaces during conversation. When you are exchanging with an Enthusiastic communicator be upbeat and smile; it's okay to be informal and take part in their excitement. You'll find a lot of sales representatives with this communication style. Enthusiastic communicators are easy to get along with and align with Thoughtful communicators emotionally. An Enthusiastic may butt heads with a Direct communicator and due to their varying opinions on details, and might not get along with a Systematic communicator.

3. Systematic (also called Conscientiousness or Methodical)

This type of communicator likes details, is articulate, needs minimal speech to get their point across, and likes personal space. When you are exchanging with a Systematic communicator be meticulous and well-prepared, avoid discussion regarding personal views and stick to facts. Engineers, Analysts, and programmers often use this communication style. Systematics get along with Direct communicators, though they like to unpack things more. Systematics get along with Thoughtful communicators too; as long as the energy in the room is kept steady. Enthusiastic communicators will have more success communicating with Systematics if they "show their math".

4. Thoughtful (also called Steadiness)

This type of communicator listens very well, prefers physical distance in conversation, and is empathetic and appreciative. When you are exchanging with a Thoughtful communicator, key in on their emotion and match it; be casual but aware of their needs; they will need more time to trust you. A lot of trainers and caregivers have this communication style. Thoughtful communicators get along with both Systematics and Enthusiastics; they match up based on pace and emotions evolved in the circumstances. Thoughtful communicators might be intimidated by Direct communicators.

Once you have chosen a communication style assessment, integrate into it your hiring strategy to ensure that you have the right communication style inside each role. Remember to study the job descriptions and ask yourself what the less tangible, character attributes are that will make each position successful.

Leaders need to study communication styles to ensure that they can understand how each part of their department or company interacts. Eventually, a Leader Most Loved should be able to use each communication style depending on their circumstances. For example, my communication style is 29% systematic, 25% thoughtful and enthusiastic, and 21% direct after years of adapting to my teammates needs. As the team's leader it is important that you are the chameleon of communication styles. When bouncing back and forth between communicating with your engineers and your marketers, it's important that you can mirror their communication style and match their energy in order to make your team as efficient and happy as possible. This takes years of practice but you can take steps towards this today! Become aware of the communication styles and identify them within yourself and your team.

Often times, professionals are promoted into leadership or supervisory positions when they are extremely talented at their specific job function. Many leaders, like me, are not naturally inclined toward people management. If you are an engineer by trade, and are now managing the office, you'll need to prep for discussions with the receptionists to make sure you address their needs and, quite literally "speak their language." To become a chameleon of communication, focus on awareness, then adaptation. When finding yourself in communications where you feel a little unraveled, take stock in the moment to reflect on it later. What threw you off? After processing, what do you think the sender or speaker meant to relay, based on their communication style? Continue processing internally, and practicing. You'll become more situationally aware and can then start adapting. Part of your Leader Most Loved transformation is deploying empathy; becoming a chameleon of communication enables you to empathize more deeply with your team.

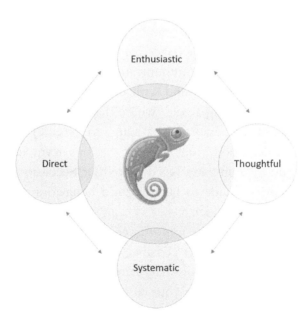

What about the Team you Inherited?

What about the team that you didn't hire? What about the team you inherited? It is very important that you become part of the existing team, but also set yourself up for success. To do this, you must have a firm understanding of your own communication style. You can only set them up for success if you know what you need from your team. Next, get to know each person and begin to recognize their communication styles, as well as how their skills and communication styles are matched with their job functions. My suggestion is to take the communication style assessment independently and spend time acquainting yourself with the results and commit to understanding each type of communication. Then, have your team take the same assessment and as a bonding activity, reveal each other's communication styles! Be vulnerable and humorous; try to make it fun for your team. Understanding your team's communication styles is paramount for ensuring the team can mesh and drive long-term growth for the company. Simply the collective awareness amongst your team regarding each person's communication style will allow everyone to communicate, with you and with one another, more effectively. Additionally, right sizing a role (where the role is either best-suited to the person, or the person is best-suited to the role) based on communication style expectations ensures the long-term success of the employee, and the company. Need more? See Scenario A in the back of the book for a guide to handling old behaviors with your new Leader Most Loved model.

To help make clear the importance of communication styles in becoming the greatest leader possible, I'll offer a couple more examples. Having a very direct or systematic individual at your reception desk may not properly serve your customers. In fact, I bet your customers will tell you about it. In a reception type role, you want someone who is willing to greet customers with a smile, ask how they are doing and make them feel comfortable as they are coming inside your office, presenting with enthusiasm or thoughtfulness. On the flip side, a business systems analyst would need to be very methodical and systematic in order to do their job correctly and accurately; as well as feel satisfied in their position. Their desire to be task-oriented and complete tasks makes them a great fit for business analyst, while reception desk may leave them (and you) wanting.

I once had an employee come into my office and close the door. She said "Listen, we need to talk. I think your boss is mad at me." This person and my boss were working on a project together and my boss, who had a very direct communication style (to which I was accustomed) hadn't been saying hello to this person. This individual was a very thoughtful communicator, which caused her to fear my boss and generated the concern that she was angry with her. My boss of course, was not; it was simply a miscommunication. I let the employee finish expressing their concerns and reassured her that my boss was not angry with her; but that her orientation towards completion tends to make her communications very "to the point" and niceties aren't top of mind for this individual. I let the employee know that I'd address this with my boss; and I did. We all had a good laugh about it later actually – my boss had no idea that she was coming across scary! She apologized to the employee, and they moved forward easily once they understood each other. To this day, this story reminds my old boss to say "Hello" in email messages.

I had one team member who started in her position with a very candid communication style, but it was a forced behavior due to her previous position. After about two to three months with us, we had her complete the assessment again, realizing she was much more of a thoughtful personality type when allowed to return to her authentic patterns of communication. Some people are one communication style at work and a different kind at home. Some people have multiple communication styles at work, based on their attitude towards a certain task they are performing.

We had another wonderful employee who is one of the most systematic and direct people I've ever met, while simultaneously being a very thoughtful peer. Professionally she prefers to be systematic and direct, but when she's engaging personal relationships, she communicates differently. She always walked away from her client sessions with spotless, glowing reviews, but her documentation was always very succinct and concise. What the client had to say about her was always more robust than what she concluded! She actually became the office party planner – it was the perfect outlet for her thoughtful communication style in social settings. Sometimes, recognizing communication styles and right-sizing people into the correct roles can save their career. Imagine being the direct/systematic receptionist. Do you think that person enjoys that position when the communication style required is so unnatural to them? This person is probably experiencing much more stress than necessary, and probably doesn't feel very good about their position. Remember, there are always three components of talent for each position; and one plus one never equals three.

See Scenario B: Conflicting Communication Styles in the back of the book for another example.

Think about which one of these categories you fall into. Why is that? Do you vacillate between two? Now, ask yourself which one your supervisor thinks you are in, is it the same? What about your team – how would they describe your communication style? If you don't have communication style data on your team now, it's something you should invest in as soon as you're ready. It will help you understand why they perform a certain way, communicate a certain way, and how their strengths and weaknesses apply to their person and their role.

RECAP The Foundation Lesson 2: 1+1=3, Right?

1. Invest in communication style assessments and leverage the data.
2. Hire with intention. You can't change core values, but you can teach skills.
3. NEVER ignore your red flags, no matter how desperate.
4. Right-size your people into the right roles.

Reflection Question:

Which of these words do you value the most? Why? Which do you value the least? Why?

- Team, Challenge, Appreciation, Feedback, Recognition, Independence.

_____

_____

_____

_____

_____

_____

_____

_____

_____

_____

_____

_____

_____

_____

Notes:

_____

_____

_____

_____

_____

_____

_____

_____

_____

_____

_____

_____

_____

_____

_____

_____

_____

_____

_____

_____

_____

_____

_____

_____

_____

_____

_____

_____

3

POSITIVITY IS KING

The Foundation Lesson 3: Positivity is King

Gymnastics is a pretty fear-defying sport, right? The things these athletes can make their bodies do is so wild – but even Simone Biles talks about the mental battle in this sport. So how do these coaches overcome these mental battles and keep athletes loving their sport?

They use repetition, praise, and positivity. When learning a new gymnastics skill, or a skill in any sport for that matter, we start with the simple, core components, and build on them. The coach works with them on a core skill, offering a few corrections, and perhaps even providing a modification while they master this first progression. Then, the athlete is ready for the next progression. And the next. The coach progressively adds mastery into the skill, building on growth by encouraging, applying incremental change, and continued repetition. By the time the athlete is ready to perform the skill, they've already done it two hundred times, have memorized the body positions, and feel good about taking it to the high beam, the stage, or the field of play. Let's say our gymnast is prepping for a new tumbling pass on floor. The coach and the athlete agree this pass is what judges expect to see at this level, and they begin working it up. But by the time the athlete has gotten to the second or third progression, they decide this isn't the right pass for this athlete right now and make a modification. It's worth the same or similar amount of points and is better suited to the individual. It's not a knock against the athlete's skill; it ensures that we get the highest score possible on this event; which is best for the individual and the team. Next week when that gymnast walks out on the floor in competition, we know we can count on a solid score to carry the team to the podium and that the athlete will feel confident in their delivery.

I like to think of myself as a coach, and not a manager. My goal is to nurture the employee's growth; find their potential and unlock it, unleash it. Coaching is where I first tapped into leadership techniques, and as my role models showed me, I would show my employees undying positivity. No matter how terrible the contract, how bad the weather, how horrid the review; I find the positive. Eternal optimist; I've been called. I've been nicknamed Sunshine and Cheerleader by my team. The nicknames may sound silly but the impression that I radiate to my team is not by mistake. They should see you as a source of light and truth, constantly. This doesn't mean you need to be a giggly, flamboyant flamingo – it means they can count on your positivity to remind them of why we are here and your coaching to keep them level-headed.

Being a coach means we use constructive criticism and incremental progressions to invoke growth, but we always deliver it in a positive way. If Positivity is King, he's wearing a crown called Reality. In other words, as a leader, we should always speak realistically, but we should deliver the realistic messaging to our team with candor, positivity, and a can-do attitude. You might giggle at the name of this next method; I promise I didn't come up with it – it's a phrase from a past boss that stuck with me because of how memorable it is! The method I deploy is called Kiss 'em, Spank 'em, Kiss 'em. It's used to deliver constructive criticism in a thoughtful way. You can deploy this method verbally or in writing. It's effective in both and allows you to deliver hard messaging with a decent dose of compassion and an overall tone of positivity. It's a matter of training your brain to format your speech (or sentences) a certain way. It's perceived positively by the recipient but still sticks. Please do not actually kiss or spank anyone while implementing these tips and tricks – it's a metaphor!

As bubbly as I can be I do have a candid communication style, especially in writing. I have to remind myself to soften it up to avoid scaring others away from having a conversation with me. Direct is often a great communication style, but part of the Leader Most Loved Transformation is adapting to others. Sometimes it's little things, like forgetting to say hello in an email or running into someone in the supermarket and forgetting to ask how they are doing. This is the beginning of what I call the "word sandwich". If you have a candid side like I do, this speaking method will be very helpful to you as you become the communication chameleon; the leader who can talk to all.

Kiss 'em, Spank 'em, Kiss 'em Undressed.

No need to blush! Kiss 'em, Spank 'em, Kiss 'em is a method of speech where you sandwich the pertinent components of your conversation topic in between incidental conversation subtopics. As a manager, I use this method to deliver hard pieces of information while maintaining a positive theme throughout the entire conversation.

Let's use a simple example – you are sending a follow up email to an employee, summarizing the details of your meeting.

Tom, thanks for meeting with me. We discussed your excellence in SEO (*KISS), your need to improve in SMO (*SPANK), and lastly, your *continued improvement in SEM (*KISS). Through our conversation, we developed the following plan: ...*

Pretty simple thought process, right? What this allows you to do is convey important information or critique, without disheartening your team. When using this method, it is important to stay on task while delivering the important critique or difficult information. It's easy to get lost in the flowers and forget the fertilizer if you don't pay attention. Remember this method is used to help you deliver hard information; it is a goal-oriented technique, so make sure that's how you use it.

Here's a more complex scenario.

Let's say you need to discuss a performance issue with an employee. We will use the example of being consistently late to work. Sam has come in late to work three days this week. In an effort to promote self-management, you didn't say anything the first time. We're all human after all. The second time, you showed interest, and instead of criticizing you asked if Sam needed anything. Today is the third instance, and it's now clear that self-management isn't going to work for this particular issue. It's time for you to open the door to the conversation.

"Hey Sam, how are you today?" *Wait for response and engage in response.

"Oh, I'm doing okay. I'm sorry about being late. My niece just moved in with us and we are having a really hard time adjusting to her new school bus schedule."

"Wow, that does sound like a big adjustment. Is there anything that I can do for you or your niece at this time?" *Kiss*

"I'm not sure right now."

"Sam, to avoid persistent tardiness, what if we adjusted your start time to 9 a.m.? That would give you and your niece about 30 extra minutes in the morning to help you get to work on time, and avoid the stress or panic of being late for both of you. How does that sound?" *Spank*

"Wow, actually I think that would be a huge relief right now. In the future, are we able to go back to an 8:30 start time if it's feasible?"

"Great, I'm glad that I could be helpful to you today, Sam. I hope that this gives you and your niece the time you need in the morning to start your day off on the right foot. I'll start your change order form right away and have it to your desk by this afternoon. If your circumstances change then we can certainly discuss this again." *Kiss*

It's important to note in this conversation that we didn't come to the employee with negativity. The conversation wasn't about criticism, but about discovery, and finding a solution that works well for both parties. To do that, as a leader, it's important to keep a positive energy throughout the conversation. Sometimes coming into the conversation very directly can be effective, but the fact of the matter is your employee probably already knows that this morning stunk, and they are just as unhappy about it as you are. In this example, the team member self-identified the tardiness issue without the supervisor even having to bring it up. Usually, when something goes out of whack at work, it's because something went out of whack at home. I find that empathizing with your team (face it, we've all been there!) gets us farther in the long run. It's also important to note that the manager formulated next steps from this conversation. This shows that the manager is reliable, accountable and the Leader Most Loved demonstrating this to the employee will promote mutual feelings, meaning that, in the future, they will try to be reliable and accountable, because it's a situation they felt safe in. In this Kiss 'em, Spank 'em, Kiss 'em, we presented the issue and immediately followed it with a solution, leaving the employee with the option to accept it or propose an alternative. The decision-making power is still in the employee's hands but guided by their manager. In the "Spank 'em" part of this example, I was able to use candid language to identify the issue; followed by a mutually beneficial solution.

Lastly, not noted in the dialogue, I should have asked this employee for communication in advance of this minor pothole! My hope is that through trust and self-management, Sam would have reached out to me last week to let me know there is an evolving morning schedule in the home that might cause disruption to the work week. We could have planned ahead and completely avoided Sam's stress! Staying in regular communication with each of your employees is the one of the easiest ways to reinforce positivity. If your employees don't seek you out for communication, seek them. Ask them to update you, share news with you, etc. When people frequently receive positive communications, they *listen* more often and *accept* the information easier. Negative speech triggers fight or flight responses in many cases; while positive speech nurtures reception. In fact, when the brain feels stressed, it triggers the sympathetic nervous system to flood our bodies with hormones and extra blood so we can "fight" if needed. When an individual is faced with positivity on a regular basis, the brain gets to swim through the chemical serotonin, which makes us feel happy, calm, focused, and stable.

Another way I recognize the power of positivity is by leveraging individual strengths. Let's say you run a help desk call center and Sandra is really good at system reboots but not so great at resetting passwords. You've tried time and time again to push those tickets through her, but it never seems to work out. You can use this as an opportunity to specialize Sandra into the reboot area and maybe it makes more sense to route the password reset tickets through Bill, who's rather proficient at them. Using this Strengths Strategy, you are increasing productivity and decreasing turn-around-time for at least two team members by leveraging their strengths and acknowledging weaknesses; as well as limiting the team's exposure to the frailty. When it's possible, allowing your team to work on the job functions they are strongest at will make your team as efficient and happy as possible.

There are situations where this can be hurtful to the team, as well as Sandra. If Sandra's inability to complete password reset tickets is a hindrance or burden to the team, meaning rework has to be done by others to accommodate Sandra's inability to perform these, other team members could begin to resent her and you. Additionally, in this particular scenario, Sandra will be ineligible for a promotion to

Tier II without mastering these tickets. Mitigate this by setting goals and committing timelines for improvement in this area for Sandra (use a Performance Improvement Plan if required). Work with Sandra 1:1 to understand what is preventing her from turning the corner on this type of ticket and make a plan. During her downtime, Sandra should watch Bill's service videos and generate questions. When she's able to, have her shadow him on his calls. Have Sandra put skin in the game by documenting what she learned or what she didn't understand and discuss these findings on a regular interval. When appropriate and within timeline, Sandra should drive the customer service call with Bill shadowing her a few times to ensure she can meet the customer's needs. Using repeated, incremental positive interactions, you'll surely help Sandra turn her weakness into a strength. As a leader, throughout this entire process, it is your role to ensure that Sandra feels positively about the learning experience, instead of feeling discouraged.

In gymnastics, our coaches deployed positive affirmations and visualization to get in more repetitions and increase self-confidence. In such a fierce sport, half the battle is mental. At the end of practice, during body conditioning, we added mind conditioning, where we would visualize our floor routines and beam routines with flawless execution. Our coaches would even send us home with affirmations to tape to our bathroom mirrors. It was incredibly powerful. Performances improved, scores went up, and athletes were happier and more satisfied with their sport. Coaching your employees through growth, combined with positivity (and praise) is key to your staff feeling satisfied at work.

Here's a few other ways to coach with positivity:

- Your mindset is the model. You set the stage; don't forget!
- Start coaching conversations with what's gone well and encourage independent reflection.
- Acknowledge all progress.

- Focus on the positives and next time rather than dwelling in the past.
- Remind your teammates of the goals and what achievement will feel like.
- Provide your team with challenges and ask them for insight into the outcomes.
- Be human; empathize and be humorous (where appropriate).
- Look for the potential in everyone.

Positivity goes hand-in-hand with goals! Having goals for each employee, each team, and even the whole company gives you commonality and, as a manager, presents you with a coaching opportunity! When manager and employee have the same end-goal in mind, the journey is that much more joyful. Don't forget to celebrate every little milestone in between. Always make goals and keep your team working towards them, with you right alongside them.

The power of positivity isn't just beneficial for your employees, though. It's for you too! Being a manager is hard work; being a leader is even harder. You've quite literally signed up to carry the weight of the company's mission on your shoulders. Positivity needs to be one of your coping mechanisms and a tool you deploy to help keep your head in the game. People who maintain a positive attitude live longer lives, have fewer heart attacks, have more energy, and have bigger chances at success. Overall, people with positive attitudes live happier lives and are at lower risk to encounter depression and are more open to opportunity. They manage stress better, process their circumstances with a lighter energy and give hope to others. You've probably heard countless quotes like, "look on the bright side" or, "enjoy the ride" and the core messaging is essentially the same; being positive brings out the best in you. When you practice this attitude at work, you will try to bring out the best in others, too.

RECAP The Foundation Lesson 3: Positivity is King

1. Try coaching, instead of managing.
2. Always practice a positive attitude and reframe circumstances to pull out the positive.
3. Use the "word sandwich" (you know what the method's called!).
4. Leverage a person's strengths and make goals for everyone on your team.
5. Positivity is King; with a crown called Reality.

Reflection Question:

What area of your life could you inject positivity into? How could you apply repetition, praise, and positivity to that area?

_____

_____

_____

_____

_____

_____

_____

_____

_____

_____

_____

_____

_____

_____

_____

_____

_____

Notes:

_____

_____

_____

_____

_____

_____

_____

_____

_____

_____

_____

_____

_____

_____

_____

_____

_____

_____

_____

_____

_____

_____

_____

_____

4

RECOGNITION IS QUEEN

The Foundation Lesson 4: Recognition is Queen

If Positivity is King and Recognition is Queen, these two have an unshakable alliance. They are constantly feeding each other motivation and supporting one another; and most notably, they are having FUN. I love, love, love passing out recognition. And who doesn't love to receive recognition? Okay, there's the rare few of us who don't, but for the most part, everyone loves to be recognized. In fact, another common response I would receive when asking a candidate for employment about their least favorite boss is that their boss took the credit or made them live in the shadows. Giving recognition is a top strategy for retaining talent; plus, it's FUN. Queen Recognition casts no shade. Long live the Queen!

Recognizing your employees' greatness is one of the most powerful things you can do to ensure your team feels valued, and therefore does their work to the best of their ability. In my experience; praise can be just as powerful as a raise. You should provide praise individually, as well as in groups. Recognition is incredibly important for your team's morale, their feelings about you as a leader, and it encourages the whole team to verbalize praise and recognition as well!

When you're nurturing and supporting team members you will naturally observe their greatest strengths and see their wins. Acknowledge them! There's no win too small for you to say, "great job." I'll reiterate – make sure that you give praise both publicly and privately. If you only do it publicly, it could be perceived as showboating and less genuine. If you only do it individually, your employees will miss out on peer to peer recognition that is important for their social development. Leader Most Loved loses nothing by praising others for their great work. Only insecure leaders feel the need to take credit for the work of their whole team. Giving praise not only strengthens their belief in themselves, but in you. When a manager only comes to an employee in times of distress or when something has gone wrong, they tend to shy away from having conversations with that manager altogether. In a virtual environment this is especially detrimental because you don't see their face every day at the coffee pot or the watering hole; you have to work harder for interaction with your team.

Recognize their little wins. If you can't recognize them right away with a "wow, what a sale!" Or a "Customer X said you were awesome to work with!" write yourself a reminder to recognize it later. Maybe there's a good spot in team meeting time you can devote to recognition. If you have a weekly stand up with your team, have a recognition board. Maybe it's a slide at the top of your monthly presentation, or a picture at the top of meeting notes that recognizes Jamie for doing an excellent job on her calls completed report. Ask your team to recognize each other's greatness, too, and to share it with you and the whole team.

In our offices, we used Microsoft Teams for a collaboration tool. As I've mentioned, this concept of recognition can be even more important in remote work environments. Our company was 100% virtual for 70% of our years in business, so leveraging a virtual collaboration tool was absolutely vital. We created several channels, one for each department and one for everyone that was effectively our water cooler. In the water cooler channel, I always made sure to honor employee awesomeness. I would post their surveys, peer feedback or customer reviews out in front of everyone, so they get some public recognition for their awesomeness. No feat is too small for a pat on the back. I always paired my recognition with a meme or cute Microsoft stock image so it's bright and shiny. This is also an easy area for me and other leaders to post about their birthdays and work anniversaries. You can even schedule those ahead of time, so you don't forget any special moments.

Incentive programs are a great way to motivate and create competition that will lead to recognition, too. By this, I mean creating incentives or rewards when team members hit a certain goal, or create a light competition amongst your team members for a prize. Remember, your people are what make your business great, so it's super important to honor your people. It may seem a bit over the top to you, but you can trust that your enthusiasm is well received and appreciated! Eventually, other teammates got into it too, and would post their own shout-outs for everyone to see! Public recognition grants your employees a pleasure they normally wouldn't get access to easily. It's excellent for a self-esteem boost and they get to feel rewarded without having to brag about themselves. Recognition delivers a dose of dopamine! The team that gets recognized feels valued; and the team that feels valued stays motivated at work.

Ways to Publicly Recognize Employee Greatness:

- Verbalize and use a visual in company and department meetings (formal recognition is best!)
- Document in the team collaboration tool for all to see

- Call out on stand-up boards and in meeting notes
- Incentive programs and competitions

What about publicly recognizing an employee who doesn't necessarily enjoy all the spotlights on them? These are your Thoughtful or Systematic communicators. These two communication styles don't necessarily enjoy all the spotlight on them. Considering your staff's reception is important, too; but studies show that all communication styles benefit from recognition and praise, even if it's in different ways. When considering your "shyer" team members, spotlight their work, more than their identity. Use visuals so eyes are on that rather than on them (or their video stream) and keep it as brief as appropriate for the setting.

Public recognition rocks, but private recognition is important too. Most of my years in the field were spent in a virtual office. There were times when I had not met an employee who had been there for years, but all the same, we had an extremely healthy relationship. When we finally met in person, we greeted each other with a hug and a smile. To get to this point, especially in a virtual business, you have to go the extra mile for your people. We'll talk about this more in Part Three, but even if thoughtfulness isn't your first style of communication, this is something you need to commit yourself to doing. Start racking up those soft skills points for your employees! In a virtual environment, if you don't deploy your soft skills often, it's easy for you to become a robot voice behind that hard, shiny screen. You'll become dehumanized if you don't make the effort to show up for your people. Private recognition can be extremely simple and powerful, and when genuine these interactions can lead to mutual appreciation.

What are Soft Skills Again?

In short, your soft skills are your interpersonal skills. The skills that you can't see or aren't quite tangible. There's more on soft skills in

Lesson 12, but in the 2000s when we started professionally focusing on emotional intelligence, soft skills were brand-new buzzwords that put a spin on interviewing. Soft skills became job requirements as consumerism leaked into every single industry. This "leak" of consumerism caused us all to pay attention to the needs of people, and rehumanized a great many processes, but most importantly for our topics today, it caused us to elaborate on job descriptions – a great and wonderful revelation that invigorated the hiring process. Problem-solving, critical-thinking, communication, teamwork, speaking (or even writing in the virtual business era), attitude, leadership, self-motivation, decision-making.... starting to see these?

If you go the extra mile for your team and deploy those "soft" interpersonal skills, your team will be more loyal, more content in their role, and will have a generally positive impression of you and the company.

Let's dive into some examples. Can you put handwritten notes on their desk to thank your team members? Can you mail them a little card for recognition or around holidays and exciting life events? I buy thank you cards from the bargain section at Target and always have them handy when the need arises. A handwritten thank you note will go a long, long way for building rapport with your employees and will help them "see" you. These small but meaningful gestures cost you just a few cents and a few minutes to execute. All you need is a couple thoughtfully worded, genuine sentences before you pop that card in the mail. " You killed that presentation on Monday. I'm so glad you're on this team. Sincerely, Ashton." I buy the blank cards too, so that if you're really on the ball you can wish them happy birthday or get better soon; those kinds of notes that show you are paying attention to their lives. You can take it as far as is reasonable, but I strongly recommend incorporating snail mail into your approach. It's so thoughtful and doesn't take a huge investment from you.

Writing a card and popping it in the mail will take you approximately 90 seconds, but when your employee receives that handwritten note from you it's very well something they will keep in their office forever. If you invest those 90 seconds in holding a relationship with your team members the outcome could pay dividends, so what do you have to lose? People don't need sappy compliments either. They need genuine and sincere commentary, and it should most often be related to their work performance. Here are some more examples: "I am grateful for your hard work on the Johnson-Roberts project." "Great job on your CPC exam! Can't wait to see you put it to good use!" "I value your effort. Thank you for working with Junior Project Manager Gwen last week." If writing out your managerial gratitude still isn't your style, there are ways to make these humorous while staying professional. There are ways to make these structured, while still expressing your gratitude.

Another idea for recognition is to pass out Awesome Citations during the staff meeting. I like to purchase simple stationery products from The Knock Knock company that will simplify these for you but still help you get the point across to your employees that you care, and that you acknowledge their greatness. In the office, I passed out these little yellow slips that almost look like a parking ticket or detention notice at first glance. When you look closer, they say funny things with a checkbox like "good parking karma" or "brains for weeks" or "organizational savvy". There's a little comment section at the bottom where you can be more sincere and personalized, but these are always a great way to make people smile and laugh. They start great conversations, too.

Ways to Privately Recognize Employee Greatness:

- write letters and send snail mail
- send direct messages/instant chats
- verbalize gratitude/recognition
- use sincere adjectives and humor
- say their name when delivering praise

Praise is an extremely important component of managing your team. Again, when the manager only pipes up when something negative has happened, people don't enjoy the manager. When a manager takes public credit for the whole team's work, or never seems to recognize when a team member has accomplished something, morale will drop, and your team turnover will increase. You need to stay positive and regularly engage with all of your staff. Making regular praise a common practice is good for comradery and increases workplace happiness. When you make praise a regular thing in your office (or virtual office), tension is lower and the communication gates open just a little bit wider. If you start doing this on a daily basis, you will be breeding an environment where collaboration and communication can take root.

Now, I know it's not all sunshine and daisies, and you can't praise everybody all day long. We screw up. We are human. We miss a zero on that spreadsheet. We drop our phone during training sessions and lose the call. It doesn't matter. We are all human and there's always room for improvement in every single position. Recognize those "ouch" moments too and use them as a point of growth. Don't let the moment slip away, even if it's scary. Do it right then, or shortly after. Acknowledge the ouch. Ask your team how we could have done better or ask the individual how they are coming back from the error and make them part of the growth process. Turn every negative into a positive. Your team will be appreciative because feedback comes more constructively and naturally, instead of consequently. Work on identifying what you and your team can be grateful for in this opportunity and acknowledge what we can change. The ability to turn negatives into positives in one of the most powerful Leader Most Loved traits.

RECAP The Foundation Lesson 4: Recognition is Queen

1. Publicly recognize your team.
2. Privately recognize your employees.
3. Deploy your soft skills, all day long.
4. Recognize the "ouch" moments, too.

Reflection Question:

What's one way you could recognize your teammates tomorrow?

_____

_____

_____

_____

_____

_____

_____

_____

_____

_____

_____

_____

_____

_____

_____

_____

_____

Notes:

_____

_____

_____

_____

_____

_____

_____

_____

_____

_____

_____

_____

_____

_____

_____

_____

_____

_____

_____

_____

_____

_____

_____

_____

PART 2

THE STUDS

5

COMMUNICATION

The Studs Lesson 5: Communication

My CEO became my work wife. I couldn't wait to tell her about the weekend's soccer game and couldn't wait to hear about dinner with her daughters. Board meetings and 1:1s were our pillow talk. While there was no actual dirty talk, we did develop a professional closeness that made us a true team; we had developed a relationship.

Talking to your team is the easiest and most fruitful way to gain their respect, and vice versa. Through relationship-level communications (informal and formal) and business-level communications, I hope to portray how to develop a professional closeness with your team. Healthy communication is one of the best ways to make a safe, fun, easy working environment.

Relationship-Level Communications.

Communicating on the relationship level is communication that promotes the respect and rapport between two individuals, in this case – you and your employee. Make sure that you have a regular cadence for communications setup with some formality to it, and that you keep the informal communication flowing all the time, where appropriate.

Formal Communication Should Occur in Several Ways:

1. One on One (1:1) meetings weekly/biweekly/monthly

Your employee should always get 1:1 time with you. One of my biggest mistakes was not implementing 1:1s sooner in my people management journey. Give what time you have. Start small with fifteen-minute check-ins and tailor from there based on the needs of the individual thereafter. Some employees might need a weekly meeting with you while others may need monthly. I have done quarterly before, and as long as there's lots of informal communication taking place in between, it can work!

1:1s should have some structure to them. The employee should know what the goals for the meeting are. In many cases, I want the employees to bring the agenda to me, but, left without structure, I find that the employee gets less value from these. In a 1:1, plan on asking three things (or more, depending on the circumstances):

- How's it going?
- Let's talk about your goals (more detail on this in the next lesson).
- Do you have the tools you need to be successful?

This agenda/structured layout allows your employee to plan ahead, and for you to remain targeted. It starts with a listening format (#1), followed by joint accountability (#2), and responsibility (#3). I always use a table format (in my OneNote application) so

I can record responses to these questions week after week to see growth in conversation or use them in reflection, and quickly add notes or mark action items. Lastly, focusing on your employee's tools and goals puts you in a position of taking care. From that place of care, you can develop intimacy or closeness in a professional setting while keeping your employee in the driver's seat of their career.

2. Push communications: messaging you share directly (standardized or a BCC) to your whole team as required or expected in your organization, with no return communication expected.

Push communications are department memos, corporate communications regarding changes in expectations, updates on policies, anything you need to mass communicate. These are usually done via email, the HR system or company intranet.

3. Pull communications: messaging sent to your employees that requires communication back in the format required or expected in your organization. This also includes surveys and questionnaires.

I love using pull communications to get a conversation started. The Google and Microsoft suites offer Forms; I use them to send surveys to the employees for anything I want a mass response from. This might be something more social and fun, like surveying where the next corporate retreat should be, or something more logistical, like surveying availability for quarterly check-ins.

4. Annual Performance Review.

Annual Performance Reviews are a fun time of year (mostly). Hopefully, you get to hand out a few raises and enroll some team members in continuing education; occasionally you might have to deploy some Performance Improvement Plans or other less fun stuff, but ordinarily this is a communication cadence I look forward to! I begin the process by performing the Annual Employee Interview the month before Annual Performance meetings take place. Then, I gather my notes, reviewing 1:1s from the year, build their personal stats, and tie it all back into corporate purpose and the goals for that year. If possible, I also have them redo their communication style assessment, and review with their dotted-line managers (secondary supervisors) if necessary. Next, I complete an updated Skills Matrix (we'll cover the Skills Matrix in Lesson 7) independently. Finally, I review my department's budget for the next year and then I have all the information I need to prepare for Annual Performance Review meetings.

The actual Performance Review packet includes a summary of that person's year, followed by their demographics, stats, goals against attainment, and individual performance data based on their Skills Matrix, followed by next steps (promotions, raises, or other plans, etc.) and organizational change forms as required. You need to plan on investing three and a half hours per employee if you follow this as a template; I eventually had so many direct reports that I needed to start in early November to complete them all (Tim Runcie, CEO of Advisicon recommends just six to ten direct reports to maintain effectiveness as a manager, but you may not have a choice as to the size of your team).

Annual Interview Template:

- Insert your employee's demographics/personal information here
- Communication Style
- Vacation Days Bank Balance/Travel Percentage/SLA/Billable Percentage
- Retirement Contributions/Anniversary/Etc.
- How are things going?
- What did you accomplish this year?
- Are you successful in your role? Do you know what your role is? Describe your role.
- What skills need to be developed in you?

- Define your current strengths.
- What do you feel is company priority right now? Discuss company goals.
- Rate your level of satisfaction in your position (1-10).
- What does next year look like for your career?
- Do you have a professional goal we can accomplish together?
- Is there anything I can do to better serve you as a leader?
- Questions/Comments/Concerns?

5. Bi-Annual Soft Review.

You often hear from employees that "I don't get enough from my manager" or "I don't get my "room for improvement" remarks until it's too late". Implementing a bi-annual soft review was one way I tried to mitigate that. Every June, I would issue a questionnaire (very close to my Annual Employee Interview template but customized for the circumstances) to pull information out of my team. I call it a "soft review" due to the fact that we aren't reviewing the employee's entire performance or reviewing the budget for salary increases, etc.; it is simply a structured conversation-starter, giving both manager and employee an opportunity to touch base on activity thus far and plan for the rest of the year as needed. A bi-annual soft review wasn't necessary for all employees, however giving the employees multiple ways to communicate with you often provides them a layer of emotional protection if they need it. It also allows you to match each person's communication style more closely by providing multiple avenues to you. Writing sometimes let's an employee narrate more freely or gives them the opportunity to start a hard conversation. However, using the Annual Interview template in June and November provides me with great insight about each person and their goals, and more time to course-correct with staff if needed.

Informal Communications Should Occur More Frequently.

No-format, daily or weekly informal communications include instant messages, some emails, calls, or in-person fly-bys. These can occur casually, naturally, or intentionally. I actually intend to practice all three for different reasons. I interact casually to remain approachable, naturally to remain "human" and empathetic, and intentionally when I need a gut check or plan to intervene.

I never recommend texting, ever. Use company endorsed communication routes always for traceability, record-keeping, and reflection. Texting is a last resort and avoiding this communication method will help you respect and maintain boundaries for your team.

Remember to make an effort to communicate with your team. In virtual environments it's easy to let the informal communications go by the wayside – don't! Keep the small talk flowing. Why? RELATIONSHIPS. Informal communications are the precipice of professional closeness and a cornerstone to your relationship with your team.

Other Communication Tips.

- Never, ever give up on correct grammar and punctuation!
- Always capitalize the first letter of each sentence and refrain from using slang. Don't let this go. It's what separates you and distinguishes you and tells your employees you hold yourself to a higher standard (another reason texting is on the bottom of my list – thank you, autocorrect).
- If you need to expedite a communication, industry-related acronyms and contractions are okay; but make sure you don't create a miscommunication over chat or channels.

I had a manager come to me regarding how to document his communications with his staff, without the staff feeling like he was "keeping a file" on them. Well, the truth of the matter is you are keeping a file on them, but not every communication needs to become part of the files. I use several layers of documentation to help keep me straight, and most of it no one sees but me. I take tiny notes in my OneNote on things that I'd like to reflect on later, and those notes are just for me. During employee/manager meetings, my camera is on and I'm making as much eye contact as possible, and I'm not sharing my screen unless collaboration is necessary. Eye contact, in this case, is more important than complete sentences. After important dialogue has occurred, I'll summarize out loud, and ask for the employees help to finish my thoughts. I start my 1:1 meeting notes inside my OneNote application from a template, but again, unless something record worthy transpires, it doesn't become part of the employee's permanent record. If it is "record worthy" I save the document as a PDF and upload it to their personnel file. Skills Matrix Rankings, Annual Interviews and other "hard" documents are part of the employment record. When an employee is in a mentoring situation and details of lesson plans and milestones met are necessary for recording progress, those should be accessible, but only documentation of "achievement" is written into the employee's record.

If an employee is expressing the sentiment that they feel like a file is being kept on them, or every move is being watched, it's likely coming from a place of misunderstanding. I explain that my notetaking is a technique I deploy as a manager, that ensures I retain the appropriate pieces of information; so that I can I support each employee properly. I review the individual's communication style to help me understand what this statement means to them. I ensure that 1:1s with this employee are scheduled and occurring, and that this employee feels they have a voice in the health of their position. Lastly, if informal communications turn into something I need to retain or act on, I ask that the employee email me the actionable, or announce that I need to pause for a moment to retain this information. This allows me to reiterate that they can trust me, that I need their buy-in to put the plan in action, and that I am an advocate for their career. As Leader Most Loved, I want my team to understand my goal is to help them grow as an individual while we work together to grow the company; everything I do is working towards a goal. Furthermore, this miscommunication can be corrected by reminding them of the self-management philosophies we've discussed in Lesson 1.

Listening.

Your employees can no longer escape work at home or escape home at work. You might even find yourself challenged with this in our new virtual-working era. As their leader, you should equip yourself with communication tools needed to support their well-being. Reflecting on Lesson 3; usually, when work goes out of whack, it's because something is out of whack at home. Be ready to practice reflective or active listening. Reflective listening allows you to show understanding and will help you generate genuine empathy. Think of yourself as an actual mirror. Paraphrase what they say to show your understanding. Never, ever multi-task 1:1 or in meetings. It shows that you are uninterested and can even be misconstrued as disrespect. Give them your full attention.

In person, you can more easily tell when an employee distressed. Virtually, it's a little more challenging, so make sure you are attentive and engaging in informal communications, in addition to those formal communications. Avoid asking "Are you doing okay?" and try "How are you?" The prior option asks for a conclusion, and they will likely just say they are fine, even if they aren't. Ask open ended questions to determine what the next steps are to get this person back to a functional state. Is there something you can help with? That HR can help with? Do we have an employee assistance program for them, or should we refer them to council outside our company? Reflecting further on Lesson 3's scenario with Sam; if you smell emotional distress, Johns Hopkin's University professor Dr. George Everly suggests rather than trying to solve the problem right off the bat, instead, just listen. Your employee needs to know that you hear them, that you are a safe space, and that they are understood. Circle back to problem solving when it feels appropriate or after the proper assistance has been provided to your teammate.

Make sure you are an "open door" for your staff. Literally, in my office, an open door meant I was ready for them to come in. If I needed the quiet time or the privacy, the door was closed; I wasn't ready. You can do the same with your Google Chat or Microsoft Teams Status. Part of being an "open door" is being open to feedback. Pull communications are a great way for you to prompt your team to give feedback. Make sure you have prepared yourself to receive it! It's likely you are going to get feedback, requests or suggestions that you weren't hoping for. Thank the person for sharing and try to be grateful that you got something back instead of just crickets. You don't necessarily have to respond on the spot; just simply acknowledge and let them know you'll review the feedback with the rest of responses and get back to the team afterwards.

I've even had some experiences where feedback was offered in a very unprofessional manner. Once, I had a newer employee hijack a team meeting when requesting feedback. This person thought his method was superior to the rest of the team's and was going to make everyone do it his way. During the meeting, I "ELMO-ed" (Enough, Let's Move On) the topic, and stated I'd follow up on the topic after we'd completed the meeting for the sake of productivity. Then privately, I thanked him for his feedback but asked that he show respect to his teammates and give time to learn the processes already in place. This time would be to see the way his team does it, try and adopt it, and perhaps learn something new in the process before trying to change it. Perhaps after further study, the issue could be discussed again in a less-offensive format. Asking this newcomer to be a learner once again helped shut off the "my way or the highway" thought-process and uncooperative behavior temporarily – and taught me a lesson. While I rarely want to shut down employees, this was one situation where your trust in the self-management philosophy can be overrun if you let it. Consider the routes and outcomes when seeking feedback. Also, consider the audience and if the communication styles in the audience are favorable for the route selected. It may be wise to break into smaller groups or change the format being used.

There's one more aspect to my "open door" policy. Allow yourself to be an open door mentally. Be vulnerable. Grant yourself permission to screw up, and to own it. Your team will see your vulnerability, and by your example will feel safe to own their own screw ups. And remember, share within reason, as much as it makes sense. Being human changes you from manager to leader.

If you are actively communicating to your employees and it's generally positive, they're more inclined to come to you in situations that require executive intervention, coaching or other growth opportunities. Keep the door wide open and ask for communication. If you aren't hearing from your team at all, something is wrong. Remember, as the Leader Most Loved, you have now assumed the position of humble servant to your subject matter experts. Often, especially initially, you need to be the one to reach out to them. It can be small, and sociable, just start opening the door with them.

It can be a quick Slack message "Hey, you are back from PTO! How was your trip?" This shows you remembered and you care.

A short Team's call before the presentation "Sal, I could use your expertise on slide 7. Will you please advise?"

If you are noticing a theme throughout this lesson, I'm glad. I ask a lot of questions. Ask, Ask, Ask. Ask questions and engage, at all levels. Asking questions is the best way to start listening, actually, because it's the easiest way to get your employees talking. My work wife used to say "there are no stupid questions" and especially in the context of leadership communication, I'd have to agree.

If informal or impromptu isn't comfortable yet (work on getting there), lean back on the structure provided at the beginning of the lesson, and switch to formal communication. Schedule a short brainstorming session with Sal. Show respect for their expertise, and that you value their time. The more you do this, the more mutual the relationship will become, and the easier informal communication will become.

See Scenario C: Second in Command in the back of the book for another example.

Communications on the Business-Level.

Communications geared toward business accomplishment, I feel, should be more authoritative and passionate. Authoritative in the fact that they are statistically founded, goal-related, and oriented around our mission. The passion is derived from serving the mission, and therefore our people. Business passion should feed itself cyclically. Remember how we touched on consumerism in Lesson 2? I feel it's important to adopt a consumer first mentality (also referred to as customer first mentality); and define "consumer" appropriately. As a manager leader, the term consumer is defined differently based on the situation you are managing. The consumer is the person you serve at that time. Daily, this is your actual team, while your team is serving the paying consumer. Developing a consumer first mentality allows you to serve the business purpose at all times, and being a demonstration of that is a model for your team to adopt; that will serve you all.

Especially in small business, it's important to get your team's buy-in on the vision/purpose. Reiterate "the why" in every team meeting, recite the mission statement at every team meeting. Don't let them forget! Bake it into everything you do so it's something they believe in as much as you do. Demonstrate the level of accomplishment in a metric other than dollars. Dollars are often lost on your staff because it can seem confrontational, like you are gearing for profit or keeping potential income from them. Instead, use numbers or percentages based on various metrics they can make an individual impact on and deliver them visually. How many customers did we serve? What is our satisfaction rating? A visual representation, perhaps a thermometer graph, might help portray how close we are to that goal. My suggestion is to deliver this information quarterly to your team. Executives and middle management should review this more often; but quarterly often shows enough growth for the team to see movement from the visual perspective. In the next lesson, we will cover business goals specifically with examples. Sharing at the business level shows transparency in management technique and further solidifies your desire for professional closeness and a relationship with your team. It shows trust, and generates trust, leaving both business leaders and team members with feelings of satisfaction.

RECAP The Studs Lesson 5: Communication

1. Use structured, formal communication.
2. Leverage informal communication daily.
3. Practice active listening.
4. Be prepared to provide emotional support.
5. Corporate communication should use visuals and non-dollar metrics.

Note:

"ELMO" is a humorous communication tool that Susan James-DeHaan, LPN taught me. Susan was an early mentor and an expert trainer of physicians and their staff. In classroom settings, she'd bring an Elmo doll and a giant notepad. Once a topic had begun to take them into a rabbit hole, she'd hold up Elmo and write the topic on the notepad to circle back to later. ELMO stands for "Enough, Let's Move On."

Reflection Question:

How can you show a team member or a loved one active/reflective listening today?

_____

_____

_____

_____

_____

_____

_____

_____

_____

_____

_____

_____

_____

_____

_____

_____

_____

_____

_____

_____

_____

_____

Notes:

_____
_____
_____
_____
_____
_____
_____
_____
_____
_____
_____
_____
_____
_____
_____
_____
_____
_____
_____
_____
_____
_____
_____
_____
_____
_____
_____
_____

6

GOALS AND YOUR TEAM

The Studs Lesson 6: Goals and Your Team

The Deloitte Millennial survey conducted in 2016 found that for the first time, the workforce (that is now primarily comprised of Millennials) prioritizes people purpose over profit. Furthermore, the survey concluded that proving a good income, being the best possible place to work, improving the skills of the workforce, and that generating and supporting jobs were top priorities when seeking employment. In other words, the majority of your workforce ranks the needs of people over cash. Additionally, Millennials want to know that they are providing services and goods that make a positive difference in people's lives. If they don't make this connection with your company, they are less likely to stay at your company. Striking a balance between purpose and profit is more critical now than ever to the success of any business. I remember in 2016 when our little company unveiled its purpose – it was a very proud day indeed. It completely tied in our personal goals and desire to serve those who serve us – into a corporate mission. Each year thereafter, we made goals to serve the greater purpose – how we would go about accomplishing the company's mission.

What Does it Mean to Prioritize (People) Purpose for a Company?

Globeone defines corporate purpose as "the higher purpose of a company that goes beyond the sole profit and orientation. The purpose is to define and deliver a long-term value – creating promise, either in the company's local environment or in the global market environment, that is directly related to the company's value creation." To summarize, your workforce needs to know the reason for business. Profit can't be the only reason for business; there has to be a greater purpose that motivates the owner, the CEO or the board. Perhaps it's a commitment to reduce our carbon footprint from a trucking company, or a small carpentry company who wants everyone to have a piece of art in their home. Once we have our purpose defined, we create goals to help us accomplish it.

Making goals for the business at the executive, middle, and ground level is very important culturally and operationally. You can unite the team once a common goal is understood. Typically, the executive goals are for the operational performance of the business and include financials and growth strategies. More recently, they may also serve social, cultural, or ethical purposes. You have probably seen Bombas commercials – for every pair of socks or underwear you buy, they donate one to a homeless institution to serve our at-risk population. They might have a goal to increase revenue by 20% this year; and therefore donating 9 million more undergarments than the year before. Their goals feed back into their greater purpose, their mission. You, as your team's Leader Most Loved will need to know these, understand them and should be responsible for tying them into the work your department does. Then, I challenge you to take it one step further and tie them into each individual employee. Doing this brings each of your team members' individual purpose and pride in making that goal happen.

Let's Break It Down.

Let's play with an example purpose with goals. This year's goals are to cut overhead costs by 2%, increase revenue by 4% and our purpose is "leave no trace" (an idea that we will sustain the environment for future generations by lessoning our impact on nature).

We'll start with that cutting overhead costs by 2% goal. As a leader, you will often have to deal with resource reductions or other similar cuts, which is why we'll dive into some strategies in detail here. This way you won't be caught off guard when, as Leader Most Loved, you have to deal with any dreadful cutbacks. Begin by speaking with your manager or leader on why we are cutting overhead costs. What changed or what causes us to have this need? Let's say this year's explanation is an increase in supply expenses and we are using the overhead costs category to compensate for it. Great! Now you know how you're going to defend this objective to your staff. Goals where we "cut" or "reduce" are tougher to get employee buy-in on because it sounds like you are asking them to give something up. What's the first thing you think of when you're asked to cut overhead costs? An even better question – what happens when you try to cut overhead costs in a virtual workplace? Cutting people is always my last resort or never an option if possible. I believe it was CEO, Michael Clark that said to me once, "Business is just people taking care of people." Fears of being let go, or not receiving raises and bonuses are things your people are thinking right away when they hear about reductions. This is why it's important for you to fully understand the larger objective and be able to properly explain these goals and apply them to your team in a positive way. You need to be able to understand strategically, not just logistically why this goal is important to the company's mission. Perhaps in this case, cutting 2% of overhead costs allows us to maintain our tree planning initiatve. Furthermore, profit or revenue-based goals are particularly uninteresting to your staff; unless it means more cash in their pocket, you'll have to try harder to engage them in this goal. Tie the goal into their role specifically and make it personal. In office settings, there are lots of ways you can cut overhead costs: switch to generic brand coffee, reduce paper printing, cut down on office supplies purchased, etc. Those are pretty small drops in the bucket but they can make a dent. In the virtual setting, it gets a little harder to cut overhead costs, so I suggest a couple of things to really dig into them.

1.   Invest in your people.
2.   Observe and perfect your people processes.

In the virtual working environment, time is simply the most valuable asset you have on hand, so this is really the best place to begin. Here are a few things to consider about time.

- If your employees are healthy and well, you will pay out less sick time. Sick time, while of benefit to the employee, prolongs the receipt of revenue for your business, so keeping it to a minimum is in your best interest. Investing in employee wellness programs is a great way to ensure that you are keeping sick pay to a minimum and that employees are happy and healthy, mentally and physically.
- Make sure your HR staff is sufficiently knowledgeable on your employee benefits package as well so you know which benefits to promote to employees and which telephone numbers they should call to get more information about physical and mental care.
- If you are running a virtual business, you've probably already done things like switch to DocuSign to remove print, fax, and scan waste from your people workflows. What about their time entry system or their project management information

system? Are those systems talking to each other and running at optimal levels?

- How many emails are required for your employees to effectively complete a single task? Understand those workflows and ensure that they make sense for each person's role as well as the transition of tasks between roles.

The above are great ways to reduce overhead expenses, now that you understand the company's objective and how it affects your department. Next, take it inside your department and bring the goal to light. Inform the team that they will be working on a 2% overhead cost reduction goal together, then, translate the goal into what benefits them. How can we be leaner? What tasks could we automate? Are there reports that we could be running automatically? Get their brains turning on how we could all become more effective. Take the time to document workflows and note areas for improvement that can be accomplished in budget within the year.

Also, you'll notice that we're talking in terms of percentages. Friendly reminder for newer managers; be sure you are always using percentages or fractions to communicate company goals and statuses. Don't mistake this suggestion for lack of transparency; this recommendation is to protect the manager. When you talk numbers specifically in front of your team you could be opening the door for salary negotiations which might not be a conversation you're ready to have. In groups and department meetings, stay away from dollar signs and convert your figures into more standardized units. Dollar signs are more appropriately used in one on one scenarios. I had an employee that was managing the costing in her department and after adding up what she thought she cost the company and what was being billed to the customer and subtracting what was paid to the contractors, she thought she was due for a raise. The truth was she didn't have all the numbers and couldn't see the whole equation. On the flip side, when you are providing your team with standardized units of measurement for goals, your team will be able to compare their productivity against that of the company's and retain information on how their performance impacts the company. This is great information to review during salary negotiations and levels the playing field for both manager and employee.

After you've discussed the executive goal of decreasing overhead by 2% with your team and come up with middle-level goals such as investing in a project management information system, task automation, or background business processes reporting, you're ready to tie this goal into individual goals. Each corporate goal should mean something to every single individual (and not necessarily the same thing), and tie back into your company's purpose and mission. In your next 1:1 with each of your team members, talk about how each person can help the first goal come to fruition. Employee goals should always be tangible or literal. They should be something measurable that you can reflect on in your next check-in or Annual Performance Review. Let's say it takes one and a half hours per week, every week for Sally to run her necessary department reports. If your department were to invest in background business processing, she could run these reports in 30 minutes. So, we set Sally's goal to decrease reporting time by 60 minutes each week (that's 2% of her salary in a 40-hour work week!) by leveraging the department's goal of implementing background business processes, all tying back into the corporate goal of reducing overhead costs by 2%.

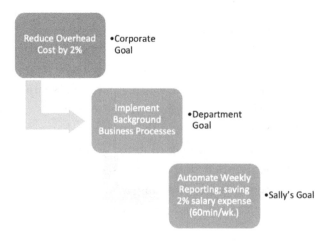

Work It Up.

Now that we've broken down a goal from the top down, let's talk about working up to that goal with your department's units. Each department has its own unique way of understanding progress and production. Do you know what those units are? Does your executive leadership know what those units are? It may be difficult to teach upward so it might be up you to convert what your people see into something the executives can digest, and vice versa. If your executives only speak in terms of dollars, or number of customers then that's the unit you'll need to adapt to or adopt. You'll need to convert your department's units into that executive metric. Let's say you manage a local car dealership and the owner wants to sell 112 cars per month. The executive unit is cars sold. Your representatives work on contacts made per day. Contacts per day is their unit of measurement. Your team makes 21 contacts per day, every day and on average they get to negotiate a car deal with 33% of them. Out of that 33%, they make a deal with one of them. There are 25 business days in a month, and you have three representatives on staff every workday. At this rate, you won't quite make the owners goal.

So, what changes? We could increase our contacts made per day, per representative to stay within the realm of feasible and accomplishable. The staff might need more training on negotiations to increase breakthrough ratio from 33% to 50%, and subsequently increase the deals outcome to 1.5 deals made per day, per representative. Another alternative could be to have the representatives work 30 days in a month, or hire another sales representative.

Are you getting handed goals like this? Do you know what to do with them? What if you work in an organization just small enough to not have these goals visible to management, but just big enough to where you need to build the team's unity? In any case, you need to study the metrics on your own and synthesize them into specific goals for your team. You can also use these metrics studies to determine where you see growth opportunities. Look back at the past several months and say, "Hey team, we've sold 1,800 pizzas every month for the last three months, but I think we can hit 2,000 if we change the third shift's start time." See Scenario G in the back of the book for what to do if you don't know your company's purpose or goals.

Another factor that coordinates directly with hitting business goals is the departmental budget. How much money do I get to promote, praise, educate, and empower my team? That way I can say if we hit 2,000 pizzas sold, we get to have a barbecue at the end of the month and invite all of our families. Or hey, I see potential in John and predict mutual benefit from him getting his Project Management Professional certification. Do I have money to put toward sponsoring this endeavor? Or, I found this really great employee wellness 1:1 session I can purchase for my team, and I think it makes sense to incorporate this into our monthly expenses – how much spending power do I have? Remember that managing and developing your people should be an important budget item, not an afterthought.

Talking about your company's purpose often is also extremely important. Bake it into each other's brains so it is always top of mind! If you work at a mega company, you probably hear the company purpose constantly and it's likely closely regarded with the slogan and branding of your company. If you work at a smaller company, maybe it's something that's said softly, that the owner truly believes in, but is leaving an impression on employees. It's something that he carries close to the vest, and that you should too. Repeat the purpose at the beginning of every company meeting, put it on every coffee cup and t-shirt, and send it out on every newsletter. It should be loud and clear and believed by everyone on your team. Employees who believe in or feel close to the mission won't leave.

RECAP The Studs Lesson 6: Goals and Your Team

1. Know your company's purpose and be an advocate for it.
2. Understand your company's goals.
3. Create department goals and tie them into individual goals.
4. Use analogous figures to demonstrate finances.
5. Know your department's budget.

Note:

Here's a bonus tip from yours truly regarding goals. Hopefully, I'm not the only one still implementing New Year's Resolutions, but having goals outside of the office is incredibly healthy for your brain and keeps you from stagnating. It helps you reward yourself for something other than work. My goals have ranged from earning my Pilates certification to knitting a blanket. Keeping goals keeps you inspired! Make sure you are refreshing your perspective and always challenging yourself to learn, try something new, or cross something off the bucket list!

Reflection Question:

Do you have goals for yourself, as manager, that tie into your department's needs and serve the corporate purpose?

_____

_____

_____

_____

_____

_____

_____

Notes:

_____

_____

_____

_____

_____

_____

_____

_____

_____

_____

_____

_____

_____

_____

_____

_____

_____

_____

_____

_____

_____

_____

_____

_____

_____

_____

7

RED PILL, BLUE PILL

The Studs Lesson 7: Red Pill, Blue Pill

In 1999, Morpheus offered Neo two choices; take the red pill to learn the truth about the Matrix, or the blue pill to go back to his former life. While ignorance is sometimes bliss, let's choose the red pill and learn the truth about the Matrix – the Skills Matrix that is. I began referencing this tool back in Lesson 1 – and this is where some of these lessons begin to tie together. If you are giving your employees praise on a regular basis, declaring self-management as your team development strategy, setting up clear boundaries, and endorsing successful working habits, you are much more likely to have a collaborative and talkative relationship with your employees and avoid the simulated reality Morpheus has been fighting. I know I'm repeating myself, but when the manager only intervenes when something bad happens, talking to each other becomes uncomfortable and you both develop a negative connotation surrounding development topics. You need to talk to your employees in their shiniest of moments, and their darkest ones too. While I attempt to focus the majority of those conversations on the positive, it's important to recognize all moments in your team member's careers. A simple, "Darn, we could have done better. How do you think?" in that moment of ouch (or growth) let's your team know you've identified a weakness, but we are going to learn from it immediately, and challenge ourselves to turn a weak or negative moment into a positive one. The Skills Matrix is a tool I use to document, reflect, and quantify each of those awesome and ouch moments in someone's career. It is a tool that illustrates growth and development and clearly articulates for both manager and employee where a person stands regarding job expectations. The Skills Matrix is a tool that shows the evolution of the individual in their role.

Traditionally, we have those quarterly or annual conversations that are about overall growth, where we can reflect on many of your employee's moments through the entire year. These moments are reflected in the Skills Matrix tool I'm about to reveal as a big part of my management structure. We review the good moments, and the bad ones during these performance reviews – but good or bad, it's ultimately all about growth. Good managers plant the seeds and help a person flourish. The roots are our experience, the trunk is our education and on the job learning, and the branches are our lessons. A great leader continues to water the tree. The tree produces leaves and branches grow thicker, into more and more until we have a full and blossomed canopy. Each moment is a leaf helping us grow our career (and life) to its fullest potential. The Skills Matrix is a tool used to tell the story of how saplings grow into great big trees.

On the top of their actual performance review document, above the Skills Matrix, amongst the name/date/role information, I usually list their communication styles from initial hire, and now. This is always interesting to monitor and measure as a person grows in their role. You can usually see a change in communication style represented in a person's behavior, and it's often affected by our experiences and our journey. For example, I became more comfortable being direct or candid as I grew as a manager, while it frightened me as a greener team member. Remember the employee I referenced in Lesson 2, that became less and less candid as the work she performed became more fun? It's a great conversation starter; a great opportunity to engage during the annual employee interview. Use this and any other inputs you've received from that person (survey data) so you can really dig into what's going to help this employee want to stay at your company, feel satisfied with their work, and thrive.

I have a Skills Matrix/Performance Review document for each position on my team built as a template, and I customize it when I need to. When an employee joins my team, I save a new copy of the Skills Matrix/Performance Review template, label it theirs for the year, and make it a living document in their employee file. It's based on the job description, so you don't have to come up with new paperwork, but it helps define how well an employee is doing in each area of their job performance. Using the Skills Matrix makes job performance more obvious and eliminates surprise from the equation. Right before performance review time, I perform the annual employee interview; so, the questions are fresh in their minds, and the data is top of mind for me too. Using a scale of one to five, I rate them before we meet to discuss. I have them rate themselves before the meeting too if we can invest the time, and then we share our thoughts when we come together. I do prefer that the descriptions of the ratings are precise rather than vague; so there is no guess work when we leave the table (see next image). The moments captured throughout the year, or the leaves on the career tree, go into the comments with timestamps so we can reflect on how far we've come, and how much room we still have to grow in that area. We make short-term goals and long-term goals for the individual, and we tie them into the big picture (corporate vision). I might also challenge an employee to rise to a certain occasion where I see an opportunity for them to grow, learn, or conquer a certain area of expertise and document these on the bottom of the performance review document. Then, we are putting all aspects of their performance on the table: past, present, and future. See Scenario E: Restricted Access to Implement Change in the back of the book for another example with job descriptions.

Office Manager Job Responsibilities:

- Supports company operations by maintaining office systems and supervising staff.
- Maintains office services by organizing office operations and procedures, preparing payroll, controlling correspondence, designing filing systems, reviewing and approving supply requisitions, and assigning and monitoring clerical
- Provides historical reference by defining procedures for retention, protection, retrieval, transfer, and disposal of records.
- Maintains office efficiency by planning and implementing office systems, layouts, and equipment procurement.
- Designs and implements office policies by establishing standards and procedures, measuring results against standards, and making necessary adjustments.
- Completes operational requirements by scheduling and assigning employees; following up on work results.
- Keeps management informed by reviewing and analyzing special reports; summarizing information; identifying trends.
- Maintains office staff by recruiting, selecting, orienting, and training employees.
- Maintains office staff job results by coaching, counseling, and disciplining employees, and planning, monitoring, and appraising job results.
- Achieves financial objectives by preparing an annual budget; scheduling expenditures; analyzing variances, and initiating corrective actions.
- Contributes to team effort by accomplishing related results as needed.

	1	2	3	4	5	Comments
	Fails To Meet Expectations	Fails To Meet Some Expectations	Meets Expectations	Exceeds Some Expectations	Exceeds All Expectations	Comments
Supports company operations by maintaining office systems and supervising staff						
Preparing payroll and controlling related correspondence						
Maintains office services by organizing office operations and procedures, designing ...						

The Skills Matrix is also helpful in assisting both manager and employee in recognizing stagnation. Variety in each of your team member's positions is important; boredom is like a stink bomb to the company's purpose. If your employee gets stuck on repeat, you better believe their quality and productivity will, too. While we review our team's job description's rarely, having the Skills Matrix to constantly remind us what kind of performance is expected, and where actual performance lies is immensely helpful. It will also help you realize where you are understaffed, under-developed, and underperforming as a department.

The Skills Matrix is intentionally templated for each position; so, each employee is equally measured. After all Performance Evaluations are completed, I compile them and bring them to the Annual Meetings. I rank the whole department based on the average of their Skills Matrix scores to help me determine who is promoted, who receives a salary increase, where departmentally we need to spend money on education and upskilling, and what steps we take as a company to refine our processes and positions to best serve our people, as well as our customers. It's also worth noting that I rarely hand out "5s" on a skill evaluation. A five means there is no room for improvement; they are basically perfect in that skill area. I like to breed the mentality that even the best of the best can seek to be better tomorrow than they are today. I have used "half scores" also if I find an employee to be between two descriptions for that skill evaluation.

As an example, let's say Annual Performance Reviews roll around and Sally is still unable to build that report your department needs. She can run it but usually gets filters wrong or sorts them incorrectly when constructing it on her own. Why is this? If you and your employee are talking regularly and are focusing on strength, throwing weaknesses on the table tends to come out a lot easier (hopefully it's come up in a 1:1 meeting). With our self-management strategy deployed, Sally probably recognizes this is difficult for her too, but may not know why, or how to deal with her short-coming. With report building as one of Sally's skills on her Skills Matrix, I have her rate herself first and then describe why she scored herself that way. This starts the conversation naturally. With report building, Sally expresses that she's improved in this area but really isn't there yet and opens the door for you to provide constructive feedback. Let her know you understand her positioning, and ask questions to continue to build her understanding, as well as your own, regarding the gap in report building. Come together on the short-coming and create a plan to get Sally out of it. Document it on the Skills Matrix form. Is there a class she needs to take? Is it peer to peer mentoring? Is it repetition or is it automation? Or is the growth opportunity severe enough to require a Performance Improvement Plan?

Performance Improvement Plans, in my opinion, are saved for last resorts. Typically, they are seen as reprimands and generally, that is how I use them. Performance Improvement Plans (also known as PIPS) are more formalized documentation, specifically on the short-coming, once the short-coming has hindered ability to perform or capacity to produce work at the expected level of quality or quantity. PIPs often dance the line between sink or swim; pass and maintain employment or fail and forfeit employment. PIPs often require HR for secure checks and feasibility, for protection of the employee and the company. PIPs are time-based; providing the employee with a timeframe in which performance will change to meet the specifications laid out by the manager. In my experience, PIPs are almost always related to your initial red flags. Skills can be taught if a person wants to learn; values, ethics, and morals cannot be changed by external forces. Don't ignore your red flags!

The Skills Matrix is effective because it provides a concrete structure for evaluation. As a young manager or new business owner I am very appreciative of having this data on hand to make sound decisions. The Annual Employee Interview and Skills Matrix/ Performance Review allows you decipher a lot of details from your people data objectively. The people data points I look to gather and track most often are: time tracked on each task, what the team excels at and how we can do more of it, what we need to grow in and how we overcome it. Additionally, I use survey data and interview data to collect information regarding the internal health and wellness of the business, as well as connection to the mission.

People Data:

1. Survey and Employee Interview Data
2. Business Wellness and Culture
3. Connection to the Purpose/Mission
4. Performance Review/Skills Matrix (Individual and Department Ranking)
5. Time Tracked on Tasks
6. What We Excel At and How to Do More of it
7. What We Need to Grow In and How We Overcome it
8. Payroll Reports

As a Leader Most Loved, one of the most powerful management techniques you can deploy is data-driven decision making. Using data, facts, and statistical intel to make your decisions gives you the most credibility amongst your team. This is more pertinent in small business where middle wellness desires, such as job stability and feeling secure, may rely heavily on your representation of the facts. When you are true to the data, you can be proactive rather than reactive. You will be confident and steady and continue to light the way for your team.

The business data points I track most often are total sales (categorized by type and prioritized by volume on the line or product), overhead costs, and progress towards corporate goals. Please note the terms used may be different based on your role and organization.

Business Data:

1. Total Sales by Type
2. Total Sales, Prioritized by Volume
3. Overhead Costs
4. Progress Towards Corporate Goals

Departmental business data should be based on the units you work up, such as number of projects, how many billable hours for your team, etc. Sharing these pieces of data with your team is very enlightening for all parties. During these moment of sharing with your team as the information is presented, you might start to get "you know what might be nice to see is…" or "how many widgets failed QC last year?" This is great! It means your team is listening and you're speaking their language, making team meetings even more valuable. Ask what they like to see in reporting from you.

My suggestion is that you collect the people data quarterly, and the business data weekly. Quantify both monthly or quarterly, based on your communication cadences. Doing this simplifies tracking for the entire year and makes year-end meetings much easier. Be sure to use visual representations when presenting the information, as the raw data is easy to get lost in. Once you've collected the data and analyzed it, map out the possibilities, pilot next steps if required, and then finally, implement change.

During Annual Meetings and End of the Year Planning, we use the people data and the business data to forecast our next year, and our next five years. This should be done very transparently amongst executives or business owners, while the information shared with employees is translated into the units of business they can consume. In asking my team what information they want to see at a corporate level, they valued that we shared information, but when we got too deep into the weeds, they became lost in the data. Keep it high-level. Following your normal communication cadences, plan to share a summarized view of these corporate data points using visuals, demonstrated in their units of business or percentages, rather than dollars.

Using a Skills Matrix in your management strategy endorses a self-management philosophy, simplifies people management by encouraging accountability, and allows you to focus on data-driven decision making. A good leader can rely on good data; and this is something you can put into place today at your office. You have what you need to get started – the job descriptions! This is usually a very eye-opening exercise for you and your team and will empower the entire business.

RECAP The Studs Lesson 7: Red Pill, Blue Pill

1. Create a Performance Review/Skills Matrix Template for each position you manage.
2. Collect feedback and data points frequently.
3. Communicate about performance (good or bad) even more frequently.
4. Communicate at the appropriate level for the audience.
5. Implement a plan (people and business) for improvement based on your findings.

Reflection Question:

What tools could you use to collect the people data points and the business data points?

_____

_____

_____

_____

_____

_____

_____

_____

Notes:

_____

_____

_____

_____

_____

_____

_____

_____

_____

_____

_____

_____

_____

_____

_____

_____

_____

_____

_____

_____

_____

_____

_____

_____

_____

_____

8

TAKE ME TO TAHITI

The Studs Lesson 8: Take me to Tahiti

Creating successful working cultures is sometimes tricky. In some industries, there's a heavy misconception that working virtually means you're not wearing pants and you're sitting on the couch. If we turn the clock back ten years, the perception was that the work-from-homers were vampires and could go a full week without donning a bra (guilty). Maybe you're on a beach in a lawn chair with your laptop in your lap and your toes in the sand – it could work... I once even encountered a man mowing his lawn during our conference call (it so didn't work). These scenarios are great in certain circumstances, but it's important that you set expectations and create some boundaries. I once described to a new team member that our virtual office was indeed a real office. When you walk past me going to the restroom,

I still want you to say hello to me. Go ahead and pop your head into my Teams chat; I'm really here, in my office, right next to you – even if it's 2000 miles away.

Now I'll specify, I'm talking about salaried employees and members of a professional team, not gig workers (those who work project-based or contract-based versus being a salaried employee). Gig work expectations really are different and that's okay. Don't get me wrong, there is a perfect time and a place for all of it. Some days in my home office are meant for sports bras and yoga pants, but not the ones where my camera is on and I'm presenting in front of the team. I may plan to work a day where I can do nothing but run my reports, create templates, and prepare presentations, so that I could work by the pool on my last day of my vacation. No matter what environment your team is working in, and whether your office is in person or remote, the culture of the workplace is your responsibility to cultivate as Leader Most Loved. The key principles in this lesson are how to set healthy working boundaries and maintain a healthy culture while doing it.

It's extremely important that you set boundaries and that your employees know your expectations. It's for the health of the employee, as well as your relationship with them, and the stability of the workplace overall. It's part of setting expectations when your team members are hired. It's part of assumptions for job performance, efficacy, and production. During interviews, I like to ask, what do you want your working parameters to be? I mean it quite literally – which brackets do we need to operate inside of to make sure your team members are successful in their positions. Merry what the company requires with what the employee needs in order to finalize the parameters. It's a huge red flag for me when applicants say that they're available for 12 hours a day. I do not want you for 12 hours per day. I don't even want you for 10. I want you for the eight hours a day we're committing to pay you for. I don't care which way you slice it, you need to be available and at your desk to take that phone call, or blow that customer away with your product knowledge, or rock that training session, or make that report shine and sparkle between 7 and 4 every day. It's about communication, and it's about being reliable, real-time, not about working a ton of extra hours.

Whatever your virtual or in person office parameters are, make sure you set them, and that they're understood. Blurry lines frustrate you as a manager and ultimately set unhealthy precedent for the employee. Let's face it, it's not healthy for anyone to be working 12 hours a day, every day. And that might mean they're in and out of their office... that can translate to lost time and productivity for the company so setting these boundaries is extremely important for both sides of the conversation. In the "I work 12-hour days" instance, his desire to overwork was beaten into him in a previous role, where the flexibility he needed to be successful outside the office just wasn't available. In reality, his 12-hours a day included conference calls in the car and emailing while cooking breakfast – riddled with genuine inefficiency. It had nothing to do with lack of effort, but rather lack of boundaries. This individual was a single parent that needed to take his child to and from private school, every day on his own. Our company was working in all U.S. time zones so we were able to provide more structure to his day, creating working parameters. His needs were very real, and I wanted to be part of his support system. We took the proposed 12-hour workday out of the equation by starting his workday an hour earlier with two breaks; essentially; his workday was broken into three shifts. He was instructed to clock in at the expected hour, and clock completely out at the end of the shift. This way when he got off work, he was really off work. He clocked out for the day and went and picked up his child. He was Dad. No worries about having to scramble back to his desk and finish his work or catch another teammate off hours trying to play catch-up. He ate dinner with his kiddo, and they did homework together, and went to soccer practice (I call this compartmentalizing; a topic we will cover in detail in Lesson 12). This improved our relationship and his home life; he called it "freedom." We could count on him at work to be where he said he would, when he said he would. Hello

Communication, Goodbye Frustration! Overcoming this required an understanding of expectations, a change of mindset, continued communication, and regular reiteration on both of our parts.

Because of the opportunity for remote work, the lines between work and vacation have been blurred. Someone requested: "I'm going to Tahiti for two weeks and would like to work from there." It is great they are taking time to travel, and I love that they're asking because it means they care about their work, but let's talk about it. I want them to take an actual vacation. We take vacations to get away from the routine and take a break. Vacations prevent employee burnout and increase overall productivity and happiness when they return. I want them to clock out and leave that computer in the hotel room, so let's make a plan that fits both of our needs. If the employee is working from Tahiti for two weeks, they are probably sitting by the pool with their feet in the water, not able to talk on their headset because there's too much background noise around them (which means lost productivity for the company). *It also means they aren't fully enjoying the pool.* Set those boundaries. If they're going to Tahiti for 2 weeks, perhaps I'd suggest only work 3 days while there, and then use paid time off for the rest (these aren't one size fits all solutions, but ones you and your company will generate as your culture develops).

I had another team member who went on vacation and planned to work 7 to 8 a.m. every day just to make sure she stayed on top of customer communications. Instead, I proposed we make a pre-vacation coverage plan. That way, she wouldn't be doing or causing double work, we've protected the company's time clock, and allowed that employee to actually vacation without thinking about work every morning and rushing through tasks. After all, the definition of vacation is "an extended period of leisure" – work shouldn't overtake that. There's lots of ways you could work this out, but ultimately setting boundaries allows the employee to have healthy division of their work-life and home-life. This also ensures the company has the productivity required to complete the work successfully.

Another situation you'll find yourself in with the opportunity to set boundaries is when your team members are ill. As an example, a virtual team member, Paul called in to inform me that he was ill, but that he would try to power through the day. I immediately recognized the opportunity to help Paul set a boundary and told him he should rest. Your employees will recognize that their health and well-being matter to you. Overtime, as you set and model these boundaries when appropriate, your employees will feel valued and your people outcomes will improve.

I had another employee that simply did not understand healthy working boundaries. This person was working from her friend's house on the couch, even from the car while she was driving to the charity gala. Although I love the freedom that remote work offers people, the ways she was working were negatively affecting her ability to perform her job function. She didn't have good cell reception or internet while she was in the car, she wasn't working with two monitors, and the work she was trying to accomplish required all of those tools. She was missing her customers' expectations left and right. Her lines had become so blurred, there was no telling them apart. Setting boundaries for successful virtual working is extremely important for the happiness and healthiness of the employee, the company and the customer. In this instance, the employee had transitioned from gig working to salaried employee. Expectations has been made, working parameters were selected at the time of hire, however applying it to her reality was a different story. This individual was paired with a mentor for coaching and grooming, then later moved to a PIP (Performance Improvement Plan). Ultimately, the employee chose to revert to her former version of employment; a decision that best suited her lifestyle. I share this story because as Leader Most Loved, you don't always win every battle; but we can respect the situation. The right decision was made for the employee, and the company.

The key here is that your employees should know that you actually want them to set and keep boundaries, that you want them to be healthy, communicate about their circumstances, and use their vacation time. It's healthy to be allowed to separate work from home when the day is done – and health is something worth celebrating. If the employee knows I care about balance in their life, they will feel more positive about their position overall, and feel more positive about you and the company. They will also be happier and more productive while they are at work. I will always try to come up with a creative solution if the employee needs one, but I really want to help them recognize their full potential inside and outside of the office.

The issue of boundaries and culture has been examined more closely in recent years with the extreme rise in virtual work. It's important to recognize how virtual work has changed our lives and our businesses. Often employees are more productive at home, but if the business leaders are not careful, they will burn out quicker. There are fewer social distractions in an actual home office, no water cooler time, no watering the plants or meandering to the supply closet. The reality is that these quiet but meaningful moments, taking little breaks in the office are critical for the mental and physical health of our teams (we will discuss this in great detail in the next lesson). There are other difficulties that have been brought into the employment equation specifically by the COVID pandemic and due to these factors employees are more willing to go the extra mile, or work a 10-to-12 hour day just to get in their 8 hours! It is dangerous, and risky. Burnout is a primary reason for turnover, and turnover is a huge cost to the business, so it is in our best interest as leaders to do what we can to prevent burn out. Setting good boundaries, even in a virtual workplace, is paramount to evading burnout.

The pandemic also forced many of our employees to parent at the same time they are working – it is simply not meant to be done like that as the quality of both suffers! Make sure your employees can come to you to work out a new schedule that will avoid as much stress as possible. Make sure that you are incorporating balance into your team discussions, encourage PTO when appropriate, and ensure you are fostering a sense of community at work that can outlast those burnout feelings. One of my small business clients is struggling to separate home from work, now that they are co-located. Moving business into the home broke all his healthy habits: grabbing coffee and scones after dropping the kids off, meeting his wife for lunch, playing basketball after work with his old college buds. It's difficult to create new healthy habits after experiencing such a dramatic break in the ritual, but we are focusing on the principle that work cannot and should not be the hobby, too. By setting some boundaries and incorporating safety nets, we are trying to rewrite his daily existence into a more sustainable, fulfilling experience.

A few of the methods we've deployed for him are:

1. Separate the workspace from the home space physically. Try moving your office to an area that can be dedicated to work; into an area that won't end up doing double-duty.
2. Separate the workspace from the home space psychologically. Make working parameters and stick to them. Create a routine that enables structure and allows you to live in the moment.
3. Create time for hobbies and schedule them. Invest in something other than work that will bring you joy and make you feel rewarded.
4. Schedule time for exercise and stay committed. Not only for your physical health, but your mental health, too.
5. Make time to call loved ones. It will nourish your soul and fill you with gratitude.

In addition to setting appropriate boundaries in the workplace, it's also important to continue fostering a positive workplace culture, even and especially if the team is virtual. We should treat this virtual office just like it is our physical one. We do have to make more of an effort to "grab coffee" with Sarah from accounting, but it pays off. Leverage the collaboration tools available to your organization to ensure these kinds of transactions can still take place. I'm talking about Google Chat, Slack, and Teams streams. I'm talking about intranet hubs and internet blogs. Make sure your team has resources to cohabitate and collaborate. And make sure that you, Leader Most Loved, are using and endorsing them to model the positive culture you want to see in your team.

Sometimes virtual networking is just awkward. Make it fun! That's your job as leader. Everyone is still clocking in at the same time they were before and clocking out at the same time they were before. A few things might have changed (like we're all wearing gym shorts instead of slacks) but our level of professionalism and ability to do the job remains the same. Stress the importance of exercising socially and physically outside the office. Promote boundaries as safe spaces. I just watched a commercial for a pre-made meals company that advertised their product as being for the "work-through-lunchers" – as if shucking the boundary of a lunch break is a positive thing! Avoid promoting encroachment of boundaries, and ensure your team knows that you want them to take their lunch and log off at the specified time. Ensure there are outlets for your employee to discuss their mental health, too. If you aren't aware of these factors as a leader, you will lose your good team members to burn out. In the lessons following this one, we will discuss ways to build a sense of community and caring by incorporating social exercise and physical exercise into your leadership strategy. Ensuring the mental and physical health of your staff will ensure you have a long-term staff and avoid turnover. Setting boundaries and having a positive culture are the groundwork needed to continue improving in these areas.

RECAP The Studs Lesson 8: Take me to Tahiti

1. Set working parameters with clear expectations.
2. Treat your office like a physical one even when it's not.
3. Empathize with your team.
4. Be flexible in problem-solving, but firm in setting boundaries.
5. Pursue the concept of work-life balance for yourself and your team.

Reflection Question:

What is one boundary you can commit yourself to implementing? What piece of yourself can you work on protecting?

_____

_____

_____

_____

_____

_____

_____

_____

_____

_____

_____

_____

_____

_____

_____

_____

_____

_____

Notes:

_____
_____
_____
_____
_____
_____
_____
_____
_____
_____
_____
_____
_____
_____
_____
_____
_____
_____
_____
_____
_____
_____
_____
_____
_____

PART 3

THE FINISHING TOUCHES

9

WHAT'S YOUR WATER COOLER?

The Finishing Touches Lesson 9: What's Your Water Cooler?

Remember that episode of The Office where they are standing around the water cooler and Dwight asks, "What's the scuttlebutt?" Gathering around the water cooler doesn't happen as often these days with telecommuting being completely normal – but you do need a "water cooler" of some kind.

Your team needs the opportunity to get involved with their peers, and with you, beyond the rapport, Skills Matrix, and business purpose. Whether or not you are in a physical office or virtual office, interpersonal interactions are pertinent for well-rounded mental health. During the pandemic, I know several individuals who inadvertently became so isolated, that they grew lonely and depressed. We want to avoid this for your team and create a community around their place of work. Your team doesn't need to be best friends, but it's been proven that people who have friends at work look for jobs less often.

Social Capital is one of the key indicators of workplace wellness and employee retention. It's also the basis of a fun, safe, innovative, and effective team at work. So, what is your water cooler? How are you going to bring your team together? How are you going to breed wellness in the workplace?

Do you have Microsoft Teams, Google Spaces or Slack? Start there. These are tools not only for productivity but for collaboration. Your virtual office is lacking that physical office touch, and here's how you provide it! Before I jump into the "Dos", a major don't is to make sending more emails your water cooler solution. Email overload and inbox fatigue aren't just fancy buzzwords, they're real risks to employee health, and implementing a water cooler is one way you can help manage that. Start a new channel or stream just for kibitzing. It's really important that your employees get to do this! If they don't have a safe space to do this at your business, your people are at risk of burning out and forgetting about your company quicker because there's nothing grounding them to your company. They'll go looking for a bigger paycheck for the same work. Your team needs relationships and social connections. "Work friends" means more now than it ever has!

Make a channel devoted to the company's purpose where they can contribute. Maybe you have a group of team members who love to cook. Start a cooking space where they can post their recipes and challenge each other to cooking competitions or print a company recipe book at the end of the year. Maybe you have a bunch of Peloton users. Get the plug in for the Team's stream and let them show off their hard work to their peers. Ask your team what matters to them and endorse it by making space for it in your workplace. In making space for your team's interests, you can engage your team more easily and create opportunity for them to emotionally invest in your company. This takes them once step closer to that perfect work-life balance and fosters a renewed sense of community within your department. I remember when one of my managers was added to a community "water cooler" channel. He said "Oh, man, my GIF game is on point! This is going to be fun!" Challenge accepted my friend, challenge accepted!

Connectedness.

Along with establishing your team's water coolers, it's important that your team feels connected to one another and to you. Let's revisit the Sam is chronically late to work example from Lesson 3. If you witness cynical behavior, chronic tardiness, or maybe repeated body odor, it's time to check in with your staff. Don't let red flags go. Let me be clear about this right away: you are not a therapist or psychologist, and nor should you try to be, but, you need to be able to mitigate and triage dysfunction amongst your team. When I observe a dysfunctional behavior in a typically functional team member, it makes me wonder. If you are wondering about a team member, I recommend that you reach out and be an ear for them! Now, while I listen to the team member describe what may be happening or what's caused them to be in a funk, my instinct is to solve the problem ASAP, but that's not always in the employee's best interest. Start by just listening. Let them talk it out. Be active and engaged. Ask questions and clarify. Once you've heard them out, let them know that you understand them. Sometimes, that's all they might need and by spending fifteen minutes with them now, you've saved the company countless future productivity losses. Because they know you are there to listen to them without judgement or critique, they will feel more trusting and connected to you and the team.

Offer hope and support. The pandemic's isolation presented new challenges for employers; people must have social support in order to cope with these challenging times. Make sure your place of work is somewhere where the team can feel safe and supported. Remember, don't overextend your capacity for support. Depending on your employee's needs, you may need to engage other types of programs to get your staff what they need. Your job as leader is to assess their needs, provide support, and follow up as required. You want to be a source of light in their life; and you can be certain your light is truly contagious. Your attitude as Leader Most Loved is infectious. When your team knows that you're willing to listen, understand, and go out to find resources, they will feel connected to the team as a community, and you as a caring leader.

There are several ways you can provide support once you've taken the time to understand your team. It may be providing structural support or actual problem solving, or it may be engaging Employee Assistance Programs (EAP), HR, or healthcare providers. Some smaller companies simply don't have these, but you can reach out to your benefits broker, or the company's health insurance provider to see what provisions are available to your staff. You can also reach out to your state agencies to gain access to resources. If you find you have to follow up more than twice, and the dysfunction is something you can no longer mitigate, it is time to triage to the appropriate professional to ensure your teammate has what they need to be successful. Don't drop a phone number in their lap either, facilitate a warm and safe introduction if you can. Accessing these resources can feel intimidating, so having your advocacy and persistence will create trust between you and the employee.

Remember in the previous lesson on creating healthy boundaries, we talked about helping employees understand healthy work-life balance when work and life have been blended together? Now's your chance to help engage them in activities that promote balance and recognize their need for social interaction and physical movement. Working at home changed the way a lot of people act. It is so much easier to work longer hours because they have a report to finish and while it could wait until tomorrow... why not finish it now? Why get on my exercise bike when I could sit at my chair here a little bit longer? It's important that we emphasize to our team that we get up and walk away from our desks, and experience other aspects of our homes and external communities, and we can celebrate those aspects when we come back to our desk the next day. Encourage your team to grab a neighbor and go for a walk after work. Join a club or engage in something that gets them moving their legs; this can be for their body's physical wellness, or for learning a new skill and expanding some brain cells! It can't hurt the team's mental health either to get out and about, and to do things separate from their job function. Get your team invested in themselves inside and outside the office and they will, in turn, invest in you.

It's the job that brought us together, but it is the bonds formed that keeps the team together. Social Capital is a critical component of developing workplace wellness as well as generating that sense of community. What are some other components of wellness that will help make your place of work a community where employees want to be? Actually, we've covered quite a few in our previous lessons that I'll recap for you now – work-life balance with boundaries, allowing employees to self-manage, granting recognition, and developing purpose. What are some other ways you can incorporate well-being into your team's reality?

Well-being is defined as being happy, comfortable, and healthy. Physical well-being (having your physical job needs met – a desk, a lamp, a computer, etc) is a condition of workplace wellness more easily met nowadays, but what about mental well-being? Studies show that poor mental well-being is dramatically more damaging to the business than calling in sick. Below, I will share three layers of wellness that will help you improve mental and physical well-being amongst your staff. A collection of these three layers is the recipe for your corporate culture.

1. Light Wellness – employer delivered, temporary or short-term endeavors that generate positivity and generate comradery; like pizza parties, incentive programs, competitions, clubs, special visits or guests, gym memberships, and cool backpacks and mugs. These employee happiness deployments are convenient and easy, but don't fill their souls. Light

Wellness deployments are helpful though, for younger and newer teams. Usually, the effects are short-lived but successful in the moment. They mostly serve as taste-testers to a bigger initiative, such as a demonstration of the vision, fuel for engagement in a goal, or stepping stones in progressive change; they work towards community development. They are usually inexpensive to deploy but won't keep an employee in their position.

2. Middle Wellness – employer delivered implements that fulfill employees' need, like collaboration tools, PTO, good pay/ stable income, and job security. Other implements include things like avoid understaffing, ensure balanced workloads, and moderating internal pressure. These things are a little harder for organizations to implement as they are usually more costly – but get this – long term, these Middle Wellness deployments will reduce your company's overhead costs. Pay the upfront fee, make the investment, and watch it nourish your staff.

3. Deep Wellness – employer delivered implementations of the deepest level include upskilling, continued learning, training and development opportunities, and even employer-sponsored physical and mental wellness sessions. This level is about thriving at work – and life and requires the business to care about the whole person's development. Ask your staff what will make the workplace well. There is no "one size fits all" solution when it comes to wellness in workplace communities. Does your team find work fulfilling? What would make work more fulfilling? Ask if they feel connected to your organization's mission. Tally the responses and analyze the results. This level is the hardest to implement but should become your top initiatives pursuant of total employee wellness. These Deep Wellness deployments are what fills your staff's souls and takes the farthest corporate leap. From saying to doing; from encouraging to investing; this differentiates your

business. Businesses with Deep Wellness are able to retain their staff and are able to recruit top-talent easier.

Implementing a water cooler for your staff gives them somewhere to bond, socialize, and create a sense of community. Whether your business has a in person or virtual office, these are powerful tools that increase collaboration and provide employees with a greater level of job satisfaction. Additionally, creating a plan to incorporate wellness into your workplaces enables you and your team to find fulfillment inside and outside of the office. Leader Most Loved wants what's best for the staff and that's what's best for the company!

RECAP The Finishing Touches Lesson 9: What's Your Water Cooler?

1. Use collaboration tools to maintain Social Capital.
2. Be observant and an active listener.
3. Encourage success and growth outside the office.
4. Seek feedback from your team to determine and improve your business's wellness.
5. Pursue wellness initiatives on behalf of your team.

Reflection Question:

Reflect on how many Light, Middle, and Deep Wellness implements your team has access to.

_____

_____

_____

_____

_____

Notes:

_____

_____

_____

_____

_____

_____

_____

_____

_____

_____

_____

_____

_____

_____

_____

_____

_____

_____

_____

_____

_____

_____

_____

_____

_____

10

DRINK THE KOOL-AID

The Finishing Touches Lesson 10: Drink the Kool-Aid

Being a leader is so much more about what's inside of you than what's around you. If you feel grounded, centered and well, and are at peace with yourself, it is so much easier to be a great leader organically. We've spent most of our journey together so far focusing on how you can fulfill the needs of your team and your organization, but now I want to spend some time talking about you. Attend to the needs of your body, your mind, and your soul before you embark on a journey to lead others. I learned so many lessons directly from the firehose and have been out of balance several times. I've loved my career so much, that I've sacrificed my body, or made personal sacrifices when I could have sought balance instead. In fact, the reason I was forced to take a step back from my career is because I was ignoring my body's needs; and that imbalance leaked into other areas of my life.

After I was diagnosed with Pelvic Congestion Syndrome, I realized just how out of balance I was. For years, I dealt with back pain, masking the root causes, and just putting a band aid on it. I spent hours at my desk, going above and beyond the call of duty while damning my body. I excelled in my career. I didn't realize what I was compromising. It was around this time that I realized, I knew what to practice, but I wasn't drinking the Kool-Aid – or perhaps I was taking a sip, but not finishing the glass. There are days when it's impossible to get it all in but giving yourself the grace to fail is part of recognizing balance. It's a journey, with no destination, with lots of Kool-Aid stops along the way.

So, are you drinking the Kool-Aid?

Practice What You Preach.

Do you have healthy working boundaries? Are you taking care of your mental and physical health (see Scenario F in the back of the book for an example)? You should strive be the demonstration of balance in your team's professional lives; and one day, you'll find you don't have to strive for it anymore, that these measures of care are coming naturally to you. The following self-care practices are about respecting the body, mind, and soul that lands you in a centered, satisfied place of being. Here's five of my favorite practices to help you maintain your mental and physical health at your desk and be a great example of wellness and balance in life for your team and your family. I believe that these practices will not only help you professionally, but help you find more personal satisfaction in life, too.

Self-Care Daily Practices.

1. Prepare. Begin each day with a brief internal assessment. Breathe in and out deeply and center yourself on your goals and ambitions for the day. Think about a team member that you want to engage with today. Think about how you can support your spouse today. It's often helpful to write these down or journal them as it promotes accountability and will allow you to look back and reflect on what kind of goals you are accomplishing each day, or what you're not making time for in your life.

2. Show gratitude. Thank your body and your mind for carrying you through the day. Thank a teammate for doing their best today. Thank your Creator for blessing you with another day. Read a devotional. Show your spouse, pets, and/or children appreciation. Putting this measure into practice can change your whole day around, as well as someone else's. Start looking for the people and things that make you grateful and recognize them.

3. Participate. Create, promote, and engage in the collaboration tools that you have provided to your staff. Use this as a social activity for your brain's benefit. Get to know those around you. This is a great time to share about yourself and encourage others to open up reasonably at work.

4. Set limits. Clock out on time and be there on time. You should expect the same predictability from yourself as you expect from your employees in your self-management strategy. Yes, you are going to have to answer the phone at 6 p.m. or jot off a quick email during the soccer game now and again, but let those be far and few between. Plan your day accordingly so that you can manage your work time within your working schedule, promoting growth outside the office, as well as inside the office. A good therapist once told me that you should never let work be your hobby. Make sure you can leave your desk and do something that promotes new

focus and refreshed personal and professional vision. This might be getting your nails done, volunteering, running at the gym, coaching soccer club, meeting someone for dinner conversation, or picking up knitting. What you are looking for is a personal investment that provides you reward outside of your career. This should be something that offers you entertainment, outlet, and room for improvement or new skills, and preferably something that gets you away from that desk.

5. Exercise. Make a point to move your body two to three times during your workday. It doesn't need to be riding your bike for 6 miles or anything like that, but you should be getting up from your desk and exercising your legs, hips, shoulders, neck, and heart. Give your body just five minutes to stretch or get some blood pumping. The University of Utah Health Sciences department says even just two minutes of walking for every hour of sitting can lower health risks associated with extended periods of sitting. Here's a few simple exercises you can do in your office.

    •   Time to thank your hips and tush. Push your chair back from your desk, slide off the chair, onto your knees. Place your hands on your hips and rotate your elbows towards your back and push those hips forward. Squeeze your glutes and tilt your chin up towards the ceiling. If sliding onto your knees is out of the question, you can also do this standing in the threshold of your door, keeping one hand on the door jamb to steady your balance.

- Let's open those shoulders! Seated in your chair, scoot your chair backwards, leaving your hands on top of your desk until your armpits are open parallel to the ground. You can also stand in the threshold of your office doorway and reach your hand up even to the height of your shoulder and walk away from the wall, slowly rotating to an open armpit position to open those shoulders. Be gentle!

- Let's modify the Pilates 100 to get your blood flowing! From your seated position in your chair, do fifty leg kicks under the desk. Keep your feet flexed, calves tense, and thighs engaged, squeezing all your lower body muscle groups. You can try again with your toes pointed, and if you can lean back a little, you could engage your lower abdominals and obliques! Next, let's engage our arms. Hold the arms out at a 90-degree angle, parallel to the desk. Engage your abs and push your arms down about 3 inches and back up to parallel, 50 times. Keep your triceps and biceps tight while doing this! If you are feeling good, go ahead and move your arms out to the sides and perform another 50 reps.

- Keyboard Fix – stand at your desk with your palms down, but facing your monitors, not you. Gently lean back, leaving the fingertips on the desk, and enjoy a gentle stretch of your fingers and forearms, giving those typing muscles some relief. Next, flip your hands back to normal position and widen your stance to about as wide as your chair, toes pointing forward, and depending on your flexibility, get your top half as close to parallel to the ground as makes sense for you. Tilt your pelvis back and look at the ground to settle into this stretch.

- Lunges are a great way to get blood pumping. At the end of the stretch above, you can go right into lunges to get a quick, little burn on. You can also challenge yourself by standing, again feet about as wide as your chair or more, and perform single leg lunges, alternating. A good goal is to just let your glutes brush the seat of your chair.

- Squeeze those shoulder blades. You can do this seated or perform standing. Straighten your back and shoulders; move your arms into goal post position and pinch your shoulder blades down and back, then squeeze. Repeat this squeeze ten times.

- Stretch your neck muscles. Put your left ear to your left shoulder for 20 seconds then switch to right ear, right shoulder.

If you're able to get out of your office, try and get your heart rate up to around 150 beats per minute (that's a good target for ages 20-45, for ages 45-70, try between 125-145 beats per minute, or ask your doctor!). If you don't have a heart rate monitor, that's about the rate you start huffing and puffing. Can you powerwalk down to the mailbox? Do you have stairs in your home that you could go up and down three times? Regardless of how you get your steps in, try 2 minutes walking for every hour sitting. That means after your conference call ends at 8:57, you walk to the downstairs bathroom and do a lap around the coffee pot before going back up to your office, and your 9 AM meeting.

These five self-care rituals practiced daily will promote the strong mental, physical, and spiritual well-being that is required to be a good leader, but also, a healthy human. Struggling to implement self-care practices? See how Barbra overcomes in Scenario H.

Nudges from the Pros:

When consulting medical professionals on this lesson's content, I was reminded of a couple of "what not to dos".

- Try your best to not cross your legs! Man, I love crossing my legs, but it's terrible for your circulation, especially at your desk. Don't do it! If you feel the need to cross them, it is time to stretch your hamstrings or try exercising the calves and quads. Consistently crossing your legs stagnates the blood flow in your lower body, and results in varicose veins over time. I'll repeat, don't do it!

- Avoid performing the cross-body shoulder stretch if you can help it. From the wisdom of my chiropractor, Richard May, DC, us veteran desk-sitters have stretched out that area between the shoulders enough so that this stretch is no longer necessary or could even promote back pain. If you have neck or back pain already, reach out to a chiropractor for advice. Try to keep your forearms on the desk, in front of your keyboard; with the wrists slightly elevated, and shoulders rested in a neutral (not slouched) position.

- Your eyes want to be as close to what you are looking at as possible. Resist the urge to lean forward. Try using the "dark setting" on your applications and consider investing in a pair of Blue Light lenses, even if you don't need a prescription. Usually, you can get these with just a .25 magnification and alleviate any strain your eyes might feel.

Office Ergonomics.

Wellness is environmental, too. My pre-pandemic home office is not what it is now. What worked for a 1-2 day per week workstation didn't make sense anymore when I was using it every day. Actually, Registered Occupational Therapist Kyle McCrite says occupational wellness in the office starts with good ergonomics (the study of people's efficiency in their work environment). Here's a couple of reminders to make sure you have a great foundation for wellness at your desk.

- Check the height and position of your monitors. Make sure you are looking straight ahead the majority of the time, keeping your neck in good natural alignment. Your chin should be neutral also; raise your monitors if you find yourself looking down. This will also encourage you to have good posture in general and keep your spine well aligned and neutral. Your eyes should be about an arm's distance from the monitor, too.
- Check your chair. Your feet should be flat on the ground with your knees at a 90-degree angle, the seat of your chair should extend nearly to your knee space, and your chair should provide good lumbar support. If you work at a standing desk, make sure you can keep your spine, neck, wrists, and eyes in good alignment while standing. If you feel bearing pressure, tingling toes, or are seeing more varicose veins, it's time to hit a few of the exercises above, and work sitting down for a bit. Go for a good little walk when your body starts to feel restless from sitting. A good occupational therapist might be able to give you some more tips on safe workplace practices and keeping your body healthy while at your desk.
- Check your critical objects. Make sure your phone, headset, and other tools are within arms-reach. If they aren't, stand to collect them rather than swiveling or breaking alignment.

My diagnosis made me realize I needed to take better care of my body, and that there were probably a lot of people like me out there. Then, writing these lessons inspired me to start my own consulting business where I focus on small business consulting, leader development, and Pilates-focused wellness at the desk. When building my business, I started seeking feedback from colleagues and trusted peers. I would reveal my service lines and ask questions to start tailoring my services to what people would want. When trying to develop pricing for the wellness service option, I was surprised to find that one of my peers did not find it valuable! Why would I want a 15-min-ute desk Pilates session, he asked? *Why wouldn't I just wait until after work to go to the gym?* I am so glad he asked. Pausing your workday for a 15-minute desk Pilates session is not about getting a sweat on (I mean, we totally can though!). The objective of making time for a 15-minute desk Pilates session is for total wellness (body, mind, soul). Taking a break to let your blood pump, rotate your shoulders and hips, engaging your body with mind-controlled movement cre-ates intention, reduces stress, generates endorphins, and endorses a renewed, calm focus. This is perfect for a 2:30 PM redirect, instead of another cup of coffee. It doesn't replace going to the gym at all; its purpose is to serve your whole body and mind, and help you be more productive with the time you have left in your workday. Once my boss was so stressed, she was ready to cry. I made her come into my office where there was a lot of privacy, I turned on the yoga app on my phone, unrolled my mat, and left her in there for a four-min-ute workout. It changed the trajectory of her entire day, allowing her to practice intention and self-control, giving her a renewed, calm focus. If she can do that in four minutes, and just a two-minute walk can reduce your risk of heart disease and diabetes, imagine what we could do with 15 minutes of desk Pilates!

You can see the value to incorporating wellness into your day. What could you promote amongst your staff? Now, here's a few rea-sons to incorporate wellness into *your staff's* workday:

1. Well employees are more productive, more motivated, and more satisfied.
2. Businesses that prioritize the wellness of their employees make more money.
3. Businesses that prioritize the wellness of their employees are more attractive to consumers.
4. Well employees miss less work.
5. Well employees are less likely leave their employers.

While some of this is my personal philosophy, all the wellness aspects documented in this lesson are founded in science and backed by doctors, chiropractors, occupational therapists, and therapists alike. It's worth mentioning, it's pretty difficult to be a Leader Most Loved if you haven't attempted to address your own physical, mental, and spiritual needs. Applying these principles to your life is just as important as coaching them into practice with your staff. Give yourself grace, room to screw up, and time to recover. If it takes you four cups of coffee to shake the lead out each day, or a few glasses of wine to unwind at night, it's time to recharge your batteries and refresh your perspective. Take a break, take a vacation, be honest with yourself, and – drink the Kool-Aid.

RECAP The Finishing Touches Lesson 10: Drink the Kool-Aid

1. Start each day with intentions, goals, and devotion.
2. Exercise 2-3 times during your workday and ensure an ergonomic workspace.
3. Show gratitude and recognize what you are grateful for.
4. Participate in social activities.
5. Clock in and out on time.

Reflection Question:

What barriers prevent you from practicing these self-care rituals, and how could you overcome them?

_____

_____

_____

_____

_____

_____

_____

_____

_____

_____

_____

_____

_____

_____

Notes:

_____

_____

_____

_____

_____

_____

_____

_____

_____

_____

_____

_____

_____

_____

_____

_____

_____

_____

_____

_____

_____

_____

_____

_____

11

IT'S ALL ABOUT ME NOW (WELL, YOU)

The Finishing Touches Lesson 11:
It's All About Me Now (Well, You)

Whether you are starting a new team from scratch or you are the new one on the team, a happy, healthy workplace culture and a productive team starts with you; understanding this is how you will earn your title of leader. Remember the habits that you demonstrate are the habits you are endorsing.

Workaholic? You can just throw those healthy boundaries guidelines out the window.

Pessimist? It's as much of a repellent as it sounds.

Glory Hog? Hope you enjoy your island of solitude.

I've compiled several tips in this lesson to help you be the best possible leader you can be through focusing on yourself. These recommendations aren't designed to add more responsibilities to your plate as manager; they are designed to lighten the load actually, by simplifying your day, changing employee transactions to intentional interactions and resetting corporate expectations. The outcomes should include less stress, diminished feelings of burn out, and prosperous relationships.

1. We Are All Human – Be One!

First, earn the respect of your team by showing them you are human. You should share personally, with some limits. This is how you start personal individual relationships. I'm not saying start every team meeting with what went wrong on your commute, but in those one-on-one moments it's okay to say, "yeah, my kiddo pooped on my sock this morning" or "by golly, I brushed my teeth with Icy Hot today." By you opening up the door, it gives your employees an opportunity to share. It's an Olive Branch.

An employee might ask me, "Ashton, what is that on your shirt, oatmeal?"

And I would reply "Why yes, yes it is. Let's just say getting the kids on the school bus this morning was a little bit exciting! How's your morning going?"

People will appreciate your reality because these human moments happen to everyone. Being somewhat vulnerable builds trust amongst the team. Sharing helps your employees respect you as a person who is going through the same things they are. It reduces fear by humanizing you. They will begin to see you as approachable. Find a way to ask about their lives. Monday morning, ask how their weekend was. If you see "soccer game" on their calendar, ask who won. You need to be just as human to them as they are to you.

2. Be Funny.

Use humor! My husband will be the first one to tell you I'm not funny, but I'm okay making fun of myself if it will lighten the mood around me. I always use real-life circumstances that the team members can relate to. I think Scott Christopher said it best when he titled his book *It Pays to Lighten Up (At Work)*. Making little jokes or painting a situation with extra color helps build camaraderie amongst the team; and again, reminds your team that you are a human, not just a boss.

3. Support the Company.

It's important that you never complain about the company or your boss in front of your team. Sometimes this is really tough because if you want to be a transparent leader, you want to tell the truth, and you want to be liked, right? Don't mistake this as a lack of sincerity; it's a demonstration of unity. You should empathize with the situations your employees are in and speak to the state or position of the company without negative connotations. You have to be professional enough to keep your gripes, complaints, or gossip to yourself.

There was this one really difficult contract my team and I were working on for years. It was hard. The customers were brutal. There was hardly ever any direction, and it pushed the team to their limits almost every week. Reinforce their motivation with your vision and plan. Even if you are equally frustrated, you must keep cool and remain positive. Remind them why we're doing this and what the outcomes will be. Perhaps you can identify a learning opportunity, or ask the team to point out something positive from the contract this week. Stay positive, it's your duty to them, the company, and the customer. Attempt to turn every negative into a positive. Each company will endure hardships and you'll have to answer hard questions. Share the why – why are we pursuing this, what it helps us accomplish, and here's why our executives believe in it.

4. Delete Negatives from Your Vocabulary.

Never complain about waking up early or working late, no matter which position you're in. It's just not attractive on anyone. Never complain about being tired; we all are. If you are upset about waking up early or the fact that you showed up late to work today, instead of indulging those negative feelings, leverage tip number one or two, and use this situation as an opportunity to tell a story. Never start sentences with can't or don't; and avoid sarcasm when able. It's about changing your frame of mind.

5. Social Networking.

You absolutely should connect with your team on social media, but with extreme caution! You are going to find out a lot more about your team by connecting with them on social media, and in some cases, a lot more than you wanted to know. My suggestion is to limit your social media interactions to LinkedIn where personal comments and emotions are left to a minimum. Facebook, Instagram, and Twitter are a little bit more dangerous and can even be threatening or intimating to the employee. On LinkedIn, you can and should tag your team in tradeshows, kudos, news articles that relate to your office or region, conferences and other news that will allow them to brag about the awesome workplace culture you and that person get to share. It's the perfect recipe for positivity in the workplace. It's free marketing for the company, and a little dose of fame for your employee. Leverage it!

6. You Ain't That Good Yet.

My first year in my professional position, a mentor was training me on a really big application, in a specialty suite that was really new to me. I had told her something to the effect of "Yep, I've got it, it's just like the previous suite." She responded to me, "Well, listen – you ain't that good yet." It struck me as funny at the time, but it's stuck with me ever since. Did I know the material? It really was congruent with the past suite, but that wasn't the point. She wanted me to remember that I always had something more to learn. It was very humbling and it's something I felt honored to repeat to others when put in the mentoring position. "You ain't that good yet" helps remind me that no matter your status or how many years in the field, you should always look for that opportunity to grow, and stay humble.

7. Your Hands Should be Filthy.

It's also more important than ever that you, as the Leader Most Loved, are willing to get your hands dirty. Put some skin in the game! Roll up your sleeves! Your team needs to see you do the most difficult or "nitty gritty" tasks that your team also has to do themselves.

Once, we were so strapped for staff in the PMO, I just started jumping in and helping the PMs wherever I could. I took whole projects, made calls on others, scheduled meetings, and trainings – whatever they needed me to do. A few weeks later, one person sent me a box in the mail; It had a medallion in it that said, "Great leaders inspire greatness in others. Thank you," and a card that said, "*I see you rolling here for us. Thank you for your devoted leadership.*"

When you tell an employee push hard for that sale, or present the findings and I'll back you up; you need to follow through! When that customer calls in and is peeved about item A & D on the invoice, you need to be the first one to start researching or show your team where to pull the file from. You don't need to do anyone's homework for them, but you better be willing to and know where they get their answers from. This shows your team three things:

1. You've got their back.
2. You have the customer's needs top of mind.
3. You are committed to the company's success and won't let anything slip through the cracks.

The theme of much of what I've shared with you is that being a good leader means earning your team's trust. Knowing where to go to get the answers and support your team in finding them is a massive component of earning that trust. No leader should be above the minutiae.

This principle has backfired on me once or twice; being willing to get dirty and even do the work if it's necessary on behalf of the customer and the business, I mean. I inadvertently enabled a lackadaisical response from a team-member because they knew I'd jump on it. Taper that behavior by reminding yourself they should be in the driver's seat, not you, and pointing them in the right direction rather than giving the answers to them. You only jump in like this when a gap needs to be filled.

8. To Get Trust, You Need to Give It.

Stressed isn't a good look for your team's leader. Learn to delegate and to trust. Sharing responsibility promotes loyalty and ensures that you are the most capable version of yourself at all times. There are certain things you just can't give away – we all know that – but think about what you can delegate, and I don't mean your laundry. Be purposeful, and value what your team has contributed. By delegating important work to the team to free up yourself to lead the team, you build trust, and the team will step up to show you they are capable.

9. Balance.

Did you catch that little comment I made at the beginning of the lesson about being a workaholic? Yeah, it's real, very real, especially in management positions – I know you are a devoted leader and will do anything for your team. But balance is healthy for all of us, and if you aren't healthy, there's no way your team can thrive in your house. Make time to practice wellness (mind, body, and soul) and implement boundaries so you can reach your maximum potential inside and outside of work.

10. It Starts with You.

Imagine a house. It's important that your team knows the foundation of the house rests on your shoulders, and your team represents the doors, the windows, and the roof. It's even more important that the employees know if they fall through a weak spot in the floor, you'll catch them before they hit the basement. It's really important that your team knows that the attitude of servitude, feelings of respect, and want for wellness all start with you.

If you aren't attempting to practice the core principles laid out in Parts 1, 2, and 3, you will need to do some reflection. Let's say you've gotten this far, and you say, "Look, Ashton – I'm just not this kind of cheerleader. I can't do this." I beg to differ. Let's say thoughtfulness isn't your first reaction. Maybe you'd rather cut to the chase – no appetizer, just go straight to an entrée.

How can you still exude an attitude of servitude without being a gushy mushy pile of goo?

Didn't someone really important say actions speak louder than words? This type of effective leadership I'm describing doesn't mean you can't be yourself. You should tailor the execution of these principles into what feels right for you, but I can guarantee that your team will be happier and more efficient if you do, and in turn, so will you!

- Be a demonstration of your company's vision. Be willing to explain it.
- Be absolutely 100% reliable. Always do what you say.
- Be the one to take action. Be accountable.
- Lead by example.
- Give credit where credit is due, and when it's due to you, pass it on.

RECAP The Finishing Touches Lesson 11:
It's All About Me Now (Well, You)

1.   Read the lesson again.

Reflection Question:

Which of these ten points are you best at? Which do you need the most improvement in?

_____

_____

_____

_____

_____

_____

_____

_____

_____

_____

_____

_____

_____

_____

_____

_____

_____

_____

Notes:

12

TIME MANAGEMENT IS MY SUPERPOWER

The Finishing Touches Lesson 12:
Time Management is my Superpower

My neighbor once told me to write a book on time management. She asked me, "How can you be such an involved mom and still get all this work done, find time to volunteer, do the kids sports, exercise, find time for hobbies, and still look so sane at the end of the day?" I'll tell you my secret. I only ask myself for little pieces. I absolutely can do it all, in bite-sized chunks. My superpower is Time Management.

Once, my brother said to me "Ashton, you are the most organized businesswoman I know, with the dirtiest car of anyone I've met." 😅 That's a good laugh and a family joke, but my housekeeper would probably tell you a similar story! You'll never find my kitchen dirty, but there will almost always be dirty laundry. I prioritize. It's a choice. I prioritize in all areas of my life. Just like in a good marriage, you pick and choose your battles (my husband gave me a look when he read this one). In the war for balance in career and life, we still have to make choices to prioritize what we focus on and what we compromise on. The only way I can do it all is by compartmentalizing, prioritizing, and scheduling. There are some things that simply must take precedence, at a certain time. But I always get my seven to eight hours of sleep, you won't find me cramming or staying up all night trying to get things done very often. I always try to manage my time by dealing with high priority items first and scheduling out the lower priority items. Perhaps that's a project management trait but I feel it's one everyone can adopt! For an example on how a workaholic can overcome internal objection to daily wellness, see Scenario H in the back of the book.

I once attended a Saby Waraich seminar where he talked about the Art of Delegation. He talked about knowing your worth and the value of your time. For me it was an easy analogy to make, I knew what my hourly rate was as a consultant and then, suddenly delegating yard maintenance to someone else seemed much less expensive, and was an easy decision to make. I am also an expert at the practice of compartmentalization in my life. It goes hand-in-hand with setting healthy boundaries. After 4 p.m. I am no longer working lady Ashton, I'm Mom – whole-heartedly. I focus fully on soccer practice, wrestling practice, softball and gymnastics, dinner and reading and bath before bedtime, and then kick butt again while next morning while my children are at school. Yes, things come up, but unless someone's hair is on fire, they don't stop what I'm doing. I schedule that out for a more appropriate time to focus on it.

Compartmentalizing allows me to grant myself permission to be who I am in that moment. I'm not concerned with work emails right now, I'm walking the dog. This skill is difficult, especially for busy, ambitious, driven people, but it's one I began to value very highly during the pandemic. At one point, my toddler and kindergartener were forced to do homeschool with me, while I was still working full-time from home. It became wildly apparent to me that we were not meant to do these two things at once! Moms are wicked multi-taskers; and so are project managers, but, trying to work while teaching the children at the same time was very stressful, and the quality of both suffered. I started to feel like "the mean mom"; my children do not understand what my workday looks or feels like – they just know they need my attention. Everyone I worked with was very kind, because they were all going through something similar, but I knew this was not sustainable. I started setting aside time just to do schoolwork with the kids, then setting them up with an activity, followed by a picnic lunch so I could focus on nothing but work for the next two hours. I started my workday earlier, and my husband would switch places with me when he got home from work (he was considered essential). It made for longer workdays but it's what helped get us through, because I could "single-task" and offer true focus to either work, or home life, not both at the same time.

During my workday, and yours, we are undoubtedly interrupted. I prioritize in the moment as well as the day before. In terms of soft skills, that's the ability to adapt and be flexible. It's absolutely a requirement in today's fast-paced society and while we are capable of multi-tasking, the quality of the output will likely be affected at some point. Sometimes being interrupted is not fun and can be downright inconvenient, but we pivot quickly, accept the interruption and reschedule our current task so we can focus on the new priority.

My Ritual.

Every afternoon, as I'm clocking out I review that day's schedule to see if there's anything I missed, or any reminders that didn't get touched. I then look at the next day's schedule to see if there's anything I need to plan for or prepare for or push forward from today's agenda. I put everything from events (meetings/places I need to go), carved-out work time or personal time (lunch with Amanda), to task reminders on my calendar (presentation due/respond to RSVP).

Then, throughout the afternoon as I'm transitioning to non-work activities, I continue to schedule my life, throughout the evening. I try to stay organized by keeping lists and updating my calendar frequently. Finally, at nighttime I check my schedule one more time to see if anyone else has added meetings to my calendar while I was focusing on other things and determine if that will change my capacity or agenda for the following day.

> 06:00 to 06:30 AM – exercise
> 06:30 to 07:00 AM – daily intentions, journaling/devotions
> 07:00 to 08:00 AM – get kids ready
> 08:00 to 08:30 AM – breakfast
> 08:30 to 08:45 AM – bus stop
> 08:45 to 09:00 AM – walk the dog
> 09:00 to 12:00 PM – work (see work schedule for detail)
> 12:00 to 12:45 PM – lunch
> 12:45 to 02:45 PM – work (see work schedule for detail)
> 02:45 to 03:00 PM – desk Pilates break
> 03:00 to 05:00 PM – work (see work schedule for detail)
> 05:00 to 05:30 PM – prep dinner/flip laundry
> 05:30 to 06:00 PM – dinner
> 06:00 to 06:30 PM – drive to kid's sports
> 06:30 to 07:30 PM – kid's sports practice
> 07:30 to 08:00 PM – drive home
> 08:00 to 08:30 PM – get kids ready for bed
> 08:30 to 09:00 PM – read with kids/bedtime
> 09:00 to 10:00 PM – yoga/knit/read/learn/watch/relax
> 10:00 to 10:30 PM – review tomorrow's schedule

Truth time: balancing a personal schedule and a work schedule isn't always easy. At one time, I was President of the Project Management Institute Inland Northwest Chapter (PMIINW) on one calendar, a mom and wife on another, and Director on the other. There were two instances when I straight up no showed a call because it was on my PMIINW calendar and wasn't visible to me while I was looking at a different calendar. It was embarrassing, but I learned from it. It doesn't always make sense to have personal events on your work calendar. You might not want others to see what you have going on, but in some cases, you might have to; for example, when a doctor's appointment interferes with a workday meeting or soccer commute overlaps with your team meeting time, it's best to have it on your work calendar, even if it's just marked as "busy" or "do not book". I use my phone's calendar layers feature to overcome that, so I can keep my three calendars separate, but see them simultaneously. It took me a while to get the hang of it, but it is ultimately what helped me keep it together in such a busy time of my life. Schedule everything visibly. Write it all down or type it all up – whatever works for you. You are too busy and your time is too important to save every bit of information in your mind. I promise you will thank yourself for taking the extra couple of minutes to make those beautiful blocks on your calendar.

How Do You Manage Your Time?

I began discussion of how I compartmentalize in the section above, but now I'll dive further into my method here. Start by committing yourself to compartmentalizing your day and acknowledging the many versions of yourself. My values help me create my compartments. What matters to you? What do you need to make time for? It's really important to me that I can be a mom and a wife, as well as focus on my career. Pieces of your day need to be committed to your employer, while other pieces need to be committed to your spouse, your children, your dog, your God, and yourself. Commit yourself to working parameters for each compartment of your life. Creating these compartments is a decision, and sometimes it's very hard. Some of us are very good multi-taskers (guilty), and it's easy to keep doing that, but it's not always for the best because we will not be fully focused on what we're doing, or we let work take over everything. Part of the idea of being Leader Most Loved is loving who you are in each moment. Be the best Director you can be when it's time to be the Director. Be the best soccer coach you can be when it's time to be at soccer. Initially, it might help commit you to your decision to compartmentalize areas of your life to visually display them on your personal calendar, or try color-coding. They might not have to stay on there forever, but it will help remind you that you've made a choice to positively improve your balance and manage your time well. When your intentions are physically blocked on the calendar, it's far more likely that you'll follow through with them, and that you'll focus on them, knowing that the time will come in the next block for other things.

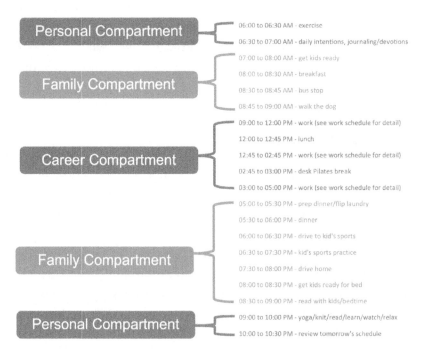

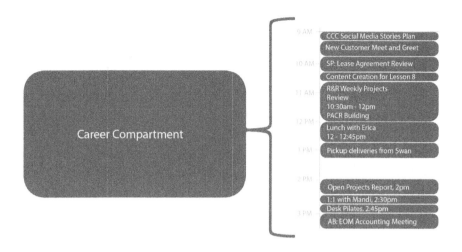

Next, you'll need to prioritize. Sometimes prioritizing is easy. At work, projects might have a hard due date. Mike Tennyson's job is due on Friday, and Sandra Lee's job is due on Thursday, so let's finish Sandra's job first. Another way to prioritize is by cost (to life, or dollars). We need a new garbage disposal and a new furnace in our home; maybe it makes more sense to finish the garbage disposal project and save up for a furnace. Time and value may also be factors used in personal prioritization. Prioritization has layers. Prioritizing may include delegating as part of the solution. At home, deciding that my time is more valuable spent gardening with the kids than it is mopping the floor or cleaning my car. At work, as a consultant I know exactly what my time is worth and that means delegating the Excel spreadsheet project to a less expensive resource is the wisest way to get the project completed.

You can start by making a list of your tasks, chores, and events and number them, demonstrating their level of priority to you. Once you have them prioritized, it's time to start scheduling into your pre-approved compartments. I leave a pen and notebook by my bed, in my purse, and on my desk to have these "brain moments" whenever I need.

My inner systematic loves this part. Putting the puzzle together and watching all the edges fit is so satisfying. I attempt to leave an hour or so of open time to allow me to be flexible and adapt when needed, or provide me an opportunity to get to back burner items, squeeze in reschedules, etc. Now that you have the template for your day-to-day life set, you know what you have room for, you know what you need to ask yourself for, and you know what you need to make concessions on. My schedule is the actual map of my life. When we press the play button on life again (or put the notebook down), you must be willing to adapt, and be flexible, all the time. That's how you will maintain the authenticity of your schedule/map, and ensure you make time for the things you need in your life. It will also contribute to your level of satisfaction in life. Being able to reflect back on your day, seeing how much you accomplished and being proud of following through; you are constantly able to give yourself that gratification and reward.

I periodically review my schedule and my goals (professional and personal), to make sure that the things I'm making time for in my life still align with my goals and what I've set out to do for myself and my family.

More truth time: compartmentalizing and prioritizing is a huge part of how I manage my personal stress. Separating work from personal into "compartments" allows me to decompress and refresh my attitude. Don't you feel better when you rest the stress?

Soft Skills Elaboration.

There are some soft skills for leaders that I believe contribute to my recipe for success. We've discussed many of these already, but I'll summarize them here again to remind you of the key traits to cultivate. In my opinion, time management is the number one soft skill needed to be an effective leader, especially in the virtual world. Taking physical walls out of the equation meant we had to implement virtual ones, which takes a great deal of discipline.

Right on the coattails of time-management, is communication. To be a Leader Most Loved, you need to be able to be the chameleon of communication; and rapidly switch between any communication style asked of you; in any format handed to you. Being a good communicator takes a little courage, and couth, too, as you are in the position to be leader and servant, mentor and executioner. If communication is scary, soften your approach to it by doubling-down on the parts you are good at, and investing in yourself in the parts you feel weak in. For example, if you feel strong written communication, and weak in verbal, try writing out all your thoughts before you speak. Practice speaking with your spouse or dog and get comfortable with your voice saying the words.

To round it out, the third most valuable Leader Most Loved soft-skill, in my opinion, is adaptability. A leader must be able to quickly swivel while remaining cool. Analyze and move forward in good judgement. The pandemic forced us to adapt in a matter of days to completely new professional surroundings, and I'll share that I've failed to adapt with grace more than once. Try stepping away to regroup, refocus, and get back in there to try again.

While some soft skills are intrinsic, other soft skills aren't always natural to people. Some of them have to be developed inside us. This isn't necessarily a class you can take and walk away with knowledge; it's something intangible that needs to be practiced and groomed; that's why they are called "soft." However, in this day and age, where working professionals rarely see each other, these skills should really be the "hard" ones! It's rather difficult to be a fully functional professional in a working environment without a medley of soft skills to help you acclimate to the situation. Here are the other soft skills that I believe are most important to your success:

- Problem solving – the ability to think critically, analyze, and resolve isn't a lost art, but in a world where Google answers everything, problem solving is an art that leaders and team members alike need to be able to exercise frequently and without prompt. Attempt to find a solution before giving up. Always seek answers based on the resources you've been given before asking someone else.

- Teamwork – many accomplish more than one. A leader's position is to recognize strengths within the team and leverage them to accomplish the goal. You don't need to be the best – you need to find the best and make them part of your team.

- Creativity – the ability to think outside of the box, use your imagination to problem solve and promote innovation inside your business.

- Leadership – sounds funny to list leadership as a critical soft skill inside a leadership book, but the art of motivating a group of people towards a common goal is something that needs to be practiced, groomed, and iterated on.

- Interpersonal skills – especially pertinent in virtual environments where body language and facial expressions aren't always part of the equation, a Leader Most Loved must have a higher level of emotional intelligence to meet teammates where they are at mentally and emotionally.

- Work ethic – I had a gymnastics poster on my wall as a kid that said, "Hard work beats talent when talent doesn't work hard". I always try to live by that saying, and demonstrate that work ethic to my children and my team. Speaking of intrinsic values, don't let anyone compromise yours. As a leader, you'll be approached with many difficult situations and choices; stay true to what you value. Only you can live with yourself.

- Attention to detail – as I advised before, no Leader Most Loved can live above the minutiae; the minutiae is what matters to your team and comprises so much of our character. Additionally, paying attention to the details is what builds your skills – hard and soft.

RECAP The Finishing Touches Lesson 12:
Time Management is My Superpower

1. Ask yourself for little pieces.
2. Compartmentalize.
3. Prioritize and Schedule.
4. Adapt and be flexible.
5. Never compromise your core values.

Reflection Question:

What are your life compartments? What are your greatest challenges in separating them?

_____

_____

_____

_____

_____

_____

_____

_____

_____

_____

_____

_____

_____

_____

_____

_____

_____

_____

Notes:

_____

_____

_____

_____

_____

_____

_____

_____

_____

_____

_____

_____

_____

_____

_____

_____

_____

_____

_____

_____

_____

_____

_____

_____

SO, WHAT NOW?

I saw a LinkedIn News poll from earlier this year that showed what people look for in their dream job – number one is a good boss and colleagues, number two was flexible working hours, and you know what number three was? A competitive salary. Enjoying who we work with and how we work is more important than what we get paid – that's revolutionary information. And now, you have the knowledge to knock number one and two off your dream employee's wish list. We all know that high turnover is a huge cause of stress for leaders and can be a big pull on your time and resources. Just by implementing some of the methods and tips I've offered here today, I can assure you that your team will be happier at work, and will stay around for longer!

So, What Now?

I've shared all my tips for becoming a great leader and building the best team. You already had the potential to be a Leader Most Loved, but now you have the tools and know how to get there. Hopefully, by leveraging my experiences, you will be able to skip to the good part and enjoy many years loving who you work with and how you work.

So now, take action.

Start with small steps and give yourself grace along the way. Work on you first. The only way you'll be able to be a loving leader is by filling up your soul. You will mess up; not every day will be perfect, and it will be hard to train yourself, but you can do it. Remember that you can't really change other people; but you can always use your influence to make a positive impact.

Take little steps. You can begin with something as small as making sure you've got a good chair at your desk. Then, work on compartmentalizing and incorporating self-care rituals. Start practicing positivity inside and outside of the office and use recognition as a tool in the workplace.

Then, take steps to implement your self-management strategy. Start practicing hiring with intention right away and begin unveiling your team's communication styles – and your own. Understand your business's goals and how they uniquely apply to your people. Create structure for fluid and productive communication as a department and a team. Incorporate your own Skills Matrix into performance evaluations and daily management. Endorse healthy working boundaries and balance; foster a workplace community where people are safe and welcome. Become a servant leader. Implement a water cooler, and practice personal and corporate wellness; advocate for exercise. Start your journey down the path of Leader Most Loved. But the path cannot begin without a first step.

If you'd like a partner in crime, I'd love to tackle it with you, too. You don't get to Leader Most Loved on your own, but by creating relationships. Gaining a mentor allows you to leverage years of experience, increasing your aptitude for problem-solving. Maybe you're a young professional, eager to take on a challenge, or a new business owner who's growing quickly; I would love to help you inspire productive, loyal teams and fall in love with your company. Ask your employer about continued education opportunities and leadership training, and if Leader Most Loved can be a part of it!

Know that businesses that invest in their managers save money by promoting positive change from the inside out.

Businesses that invest in their managers see increased employee engagement.

Businesses that invest in their managers build loyalty throughout the ranks.

Businesses that invest in their managers can expect more effective and productive teams.

One of the things I've enjoyed most about writing this book and starting my business is getting to meet so many wonderful people who want to invest in their teams, and themselves. I would love to be inspired by you. So, reach out to me on LinkedIn, or DM me on Instagram (@cadre.coeur)! Post a picture of you and your copy of Leader Most Loved and tag me for 30% off the Leader Most Loved training course! Or, visit my website, www.cadrecoeur.com to sign you or your company up for desk-Pilates or a small business coaching session. Let's embark on a transformative journey to become Leader Most Loved, let's talk about your business, and let's inspire more and more companies to invest in healthy work cultures! In fact, just for reading my book, sign up a free desk-Pilates session on my website with promo code "sowhatnow"! My goal is to enable you, and empower you. For you to be able to create a healthy, positive, trusting, and happy business organization in just a matter of months. Management will become simpler, business will flow easier, and clients and employees will all be served better, and you might just become a Leader Most Loved.

SCENARIOS

Scenario A: Team Inherited Performance Quandary

Molly has inherited a team of three project managers. Molly has noticed that unless she is in the bullpen every day, the project managers aren't pursuing project progress; but rather are waiting for the customers to come to them. Molly knows that isn't good for the business's reputation and slows the revenue cycle down. She wants to make a good impression on her new team. How should she go about implementing change?

1. Share the company's vision. Help them to understand what the goals are, why they are here, and how they are a part of the bigger picture. Ask them which pieces they resonate with, and how they think they can contribute to this goal (Lesson 6).

2. Meet individually. Get to know the employee professionally, and as personally as is appropriate for the circumstances. Document their career goals, short term, and long term. Tie their goals into the company's goals. This breathes passion into the company's vision because it's directly associated to their personal success. Ask the employee to identify their strengths and weaknesses, so you know where to provide the

most support. Make sure they know that's why and mean it. Ask for their opinion on where the department needs the most support. Set boundaries. Tell them what you need, how you need it and what working together will feel like. Finally, setup a regular communication cadence (Lesson 5).

3. Have the employee fill out a Skills Matrix with you (Lesson 7).
4. Implement healthy boundaries (Lesson 8).
5. Implement the Self-Management People Strategy (Lesson 1).
6. Use a Performance Improvement Plan as required if things do not improve with the above implemented (Lesson 7).

Scenario B: Conflicting Communication Styles

Tanya has managed a small construction company for six years and has just promoted a senior employee into a Foreman. He was thrilled about the promotion but has yet to fully embrace his responsibilities. When presented with decisions to make the Foreman displays a lack of confidence and sits on them, when Tanya prefers him to take action. He is also somewhat defensive when Tanya asks him about projects, documentation, and client communications. How does Tanya get the Foreman to accept accountability and buy into management?

1. We need to build this Foreman's confidence, but first let's build his confidence in you (Lesson 11). Start building trust by forming a relationship. Begin seeking his expertise, and empowering his decision making. Discuss the decisions with him by asking him about past experiences that will help him come to conclusion with your assistance.
2. Let's figure out what his communication style is and why it's hard for Tanya and this person to get on the same page (Lesson 2).
3. Review the job description with the new Foreman. Deploy the Annual Employee Interview to get information flowing

that's more about him rather than the position. Then, deploy a Skills Matrix and have the Foreman rank himself and discuss the results together (Lesson 7).

4. Review personalized findings, locate commonalities, and roll them into corporate goals (Lesson 6). Create unity between Tanya and the Foreman.

5. Setup regular communication cadences to prevent regression (Lesson 5).

Scenario C: Second in Command

John is the senior drafter on staff, not the manager. The team views him as a leader due to his expertise and years at the job and is struggling to respect the manager's style. This manager is hovering a lot, micromanaging, and interrupts the drafters when brainstorming. How should John attempt to address Leader Most Loved motivations without offending his manager or alerting his team?

1. Avoid dissention in the ranks! Refrain from speaking negatively about this manager but assure your team you think things can improve (Lesson 11).

2. Review your corporate and department goals. Collect data on drafter workflow and the value of autonomy and uninterrupted brainstorming sessions. Then, make suggestions to improve workflow and how autonomy and independence will have a positive impact on performance and productivity and find correlations to the company goals. Suggest scheduled blocks for brainstorming and other activities, and scheduled blocks for communication. Formalize the information and prepare to present it to the manager (Lesson 6).

3. Use informal, followed by formal communication to let the manager know that you've heard some grumblings amongst the team, and think you've found ways to increase productivity and would like to meet to discuss further (Lesson 5 and 12).

4. Present your findings and data to the manager and ask for help creating a plan to implement it. Involve them in the solution. Avoid emotional context and stay fact-based; you do not want your presentation to be interpreted as office drama or create gossip. Ask for feedback. Ask what the manager sees as most valuable to the company. Use active listening to continue to be an effective communicator (Lesson 9).

5. Be prepared to celebrate this victory from the sidelines (Lesson 11).

6. If it becomes appropriate, share your copy of Leader Most Loved. Share what you have learned or appreciated from the book and ask if you can read it and discuss it further together. There is nowhere but up to go from this conversation!

Scenario D: Change will be hard; is it too late?

Wanda has been managing the same team for four years with a more traditional management style that she would like to break away from. How can she deploy her new learned Leader Most Loved techniques, including a philosophy of self-management to her team, without upsetting the apple cart?

1. Start by working on yourself, first; those changes will be noticeable to the team. You can start with the self-improvement and self-sustaining techniques learned in Lesson 11, as well as stress management and time management in Lesson 12. Let that settle in for a few weeks.

2. Begin incorporating wellness (Lesson 10) in your self-care plan, as well as encouraging your team to take part.

3. Build a water cooler (Lesson 9) for the employees to "gather around" and incorporate "light wellness" into the workplace. See how many middle wellness components you can cross off, too.

4. Implement Positivity (Lesson 3) and Recognition (Lesson 4) when speaking to the team.

5. Speak to the team 1:1 and in groups regarding goals and start spreading purpose amongst positivity (Lesson 6). You can begin to discuss your new goals slowly with these communication touchpoints set up.

6. Study their communication styles (Lesson 2) to determine how you'll be received and who is going to need the most help to get to self-management. Prime healthy boundaries and start describing what you want self-management to look like (Lesson 5 and Lesson 8).

7. Incrementally introduce the Skills Matrix (Lesson 7) and self-management strategies (Lesson 1).

Scenario E: Restricted Access to Implement Change

Herold is the manager of the IT department but doesn't get to write the job descriptions; his boss does. He and his team have been exploring self-management principles and corporate goals. How can he continue right sizing his team without undermining his boss?

1. Start by reviewing the job descriptions you have and interviewing your team. How closely does the actual position compare to the position on paper (Lesson 7, Lesson 5)? Acknowledge and document the differences. Prepare explanations as to why such changes have occurred; good or bad.

2. Next, review the goals of the company. Does the job description still serve the purpose (Lesson 6)? What kinds of changes caused the deviation from the predicted or anticipated position?

3. Use informal and formal communication to right-size your team into the correct positions as within your power. For those positions that have separated from the proposed job description, respectfully request a meeting with your boss to

discuss further. We don't want to make new roles for fun; we want to satisfy our employees with meaningful work and room for growth that feeds the corporate purpose (Lesson 2, Lesson 5).

Scenario F: My Plate is Pretty Full

Sarah is a single mom with two daughters, ages 1 and 3, and just feels maxed out, all the time. In fact, she is struggling with motivating herself, let alone the team of 5 project managers she leads. What should she do?

1. We have all had full plate moments like Sarah's. First things first, Sarah needs some vacation, some PTO to catch her breath and decompress (Lesson 8 and 10).

2. While on PTO, there are a few things I'd advocate for Sarah to do away from her team. Allow her to reframe (Lesson 3) and find the positive in each day; while the agenda is smaller (we are on vacation, right?). Then, have the King telephone his Queen; and have Sarah work on rewarding herself for how far she's come (Lesson 4) and start a self-care plan (Lesson 10).

3. Next, let's begin what we learned in Lesson 12, using compartmentalization, prioritization, and scheduling to begin managing Sarah's stress. Right now, we need Sarah to take care of herself and her kids, before she can think of taking care of others.

4. Practice the first three steps for about a month, until it feels natural and normal, and there's a schedule in place helping Sarah look forward to what's down the road. After that, Sarah can work on a few Lesson 11 tips at a time, slowly implementing them into her life. Her team will observe these positive changes in her, and just her presence will provide a positive impact on her team.

5. After two or three months have passed, Sarah can look to begin promoting and engaging her staff (Lesson 9) and work towards a self-managing department (Lesson 1 and 2).

Scenario G: I Don't Know What my Company's Vision is

Brad is the manager of a small to medium-sized local lawn care company. He doesn't meet with leadership often, and really has no idea what goals his leadership has in mind, or what the corporate mission is. He manages 12 trucks and 16 mobile employees. After reading Leader Most Loved, Brad wonders how he could unify his team. How can he unite his staff under something he can't see?

1. Brad should start by interviewing his staff. Ask them what excites them about their position, what their favorite part is/least favorite part is; and complete the Annual Employee Interview to the best of his ability (Lesson 5).

2. Next, approach your leadership and ask about goals. Due to many variables, leadership may be uncomfortable sharing with you or be uncertain about actual goals, but usually, they can speak to purpose. Small and medium-sized companies usually are associated with the owner's personal mission or drive. Ask them what prompted them to start the company. Ask what the next big move is for the company, and where the owner sees the company in five years (Lesson 6). Use active listening and enjoy hearing your boss pour out their passion (Lesson 5).

3. From this information, the company's purpose is something that can be formalized, and subsequently goals working towards accomplishing that purpose (Lesson 6). Then, Brad can work up units to tie into those corporate goals with each individual team member. Your team wants that motivating, uniting factor! Connection to the purpose feeds the whole team's soul and increases workplace satisfaction.

Scenario H: Workaholic Overcomes

Barbra loves her career and her work; it brings her great joy to be productive. She's worked from home for twenty years and while she has some hobbies, she prefers to putter at her computer after work hours and is intrinsically motivated to keep working. Recently, her doctor advised her to incorporate exercise into her day for health reasons. How does Barbra learn to change her behavior?

1. I would suggest to Barbra we try compartmentalizing, prioritizing and scheduling (Lesson 12) to help us stay accountable for our wellness tasks, especially since they aren't our favorite thing to do. We would choose times of time day to consistently introduce exercise, and schedule them into her pre or post workday schedule compartments.

2. Beyond that, I would refer Barbra to some of our Lesson 11 topics and begin incorporating desk exercise from self-care tip number 5 into her workday to normalize some of the concepts to her. Asking ourselves for a little bit is much easier to accept! Just a few minutes at a time (2-15 minutes), we schedule exercise into her workday. Sometimes, a wellness web appointment can be helpful initially to embed accountability.

3. After several weeks to adjust to our bite-sized introduction of exercise, we can consider increasing the duration of the intervals based on the continued guidance of Barbra's healthcare provider.

Scenario I: Self-Management Backfires

Zack is the supervisor for the business analyst team and manages five. He's implemented the self-management strategy for about five months now, and most of the team is doing well, however, one of the business analysts (BA) has come to him frustrated. Sean, another BA, has been leaving all the level two projects for the other BAs to complete. This team member has also been consistently leaving the office early, dumping work on the rest of the team's plates. How should Zack address this with the concerned team member, and the individual taking advantage of the situation?

1. First of all, I would recommend that Zack be looking at productivity and outcome reports more often. If he had been, he would have noticed that Sean was leaving harder projects for others or performing at a lower level; he would have also noticed reduced productivity and inaccurate time clocking reports (Lesson 1).

2. Next, Zack should dig in. Let the person who came to him know that he values their effort, understands their position, and that they should keep doing their best while he investigates. Then, Zack should pull several weeks (the whole five months if necessary) of outcomes and productivity data and compare each BA by level and productivity. Analyze the data and summarize the findings. Consider giving praise to top performers during the next staff meeting and privately, measure what kinds of deficiencies Zack is dealing with in Sean's situation (Lesson 4). Is it truly productivity? Is it just laziness? Can it be corrected?

3. Zack should also review the self-management implementation strategy as it was discussed, as well as the BA job description before asking Sean to visit with him. Remember, self-management doesn't work for everyone. Creating benchmarks and baseline expectations may help this individual succeed in their role (Lesson 6 and 7).

4. Zack should share with Sean that he's noticed declining productivity over time, and a decrease in work complexity. Speak to the data you've studied. Ask for Sean's feedback. Ask what would help Sean perform at expected productivity and complexity. Suggest benchmarks and create goals that Zack and Sean can discuss frequently during their 1:1 meetings

(Lesson 5) and potentially avoid going the route of a PIP
(Performance Improvement Plan) (Lesson 7).

5. The clocking out early accusation can be serious (time theft).
   Zack should mention to Sean that he's noticed him ducking
   out early here and there (don't mention the other employee),
   and ask for communication. Not only does that have an
   impact on the outcome reporting Zack is reviewing, but it
   has an impact on the team's moral. If Sean can communicate
   to Zack his needs, they can agree on what serves both the
   company and the individual (Lesson 8).

Made in the USA
Las Vegas, NV
14 March 2023

69051567R00095